CW01213202

EMBERS OF THE SOUL

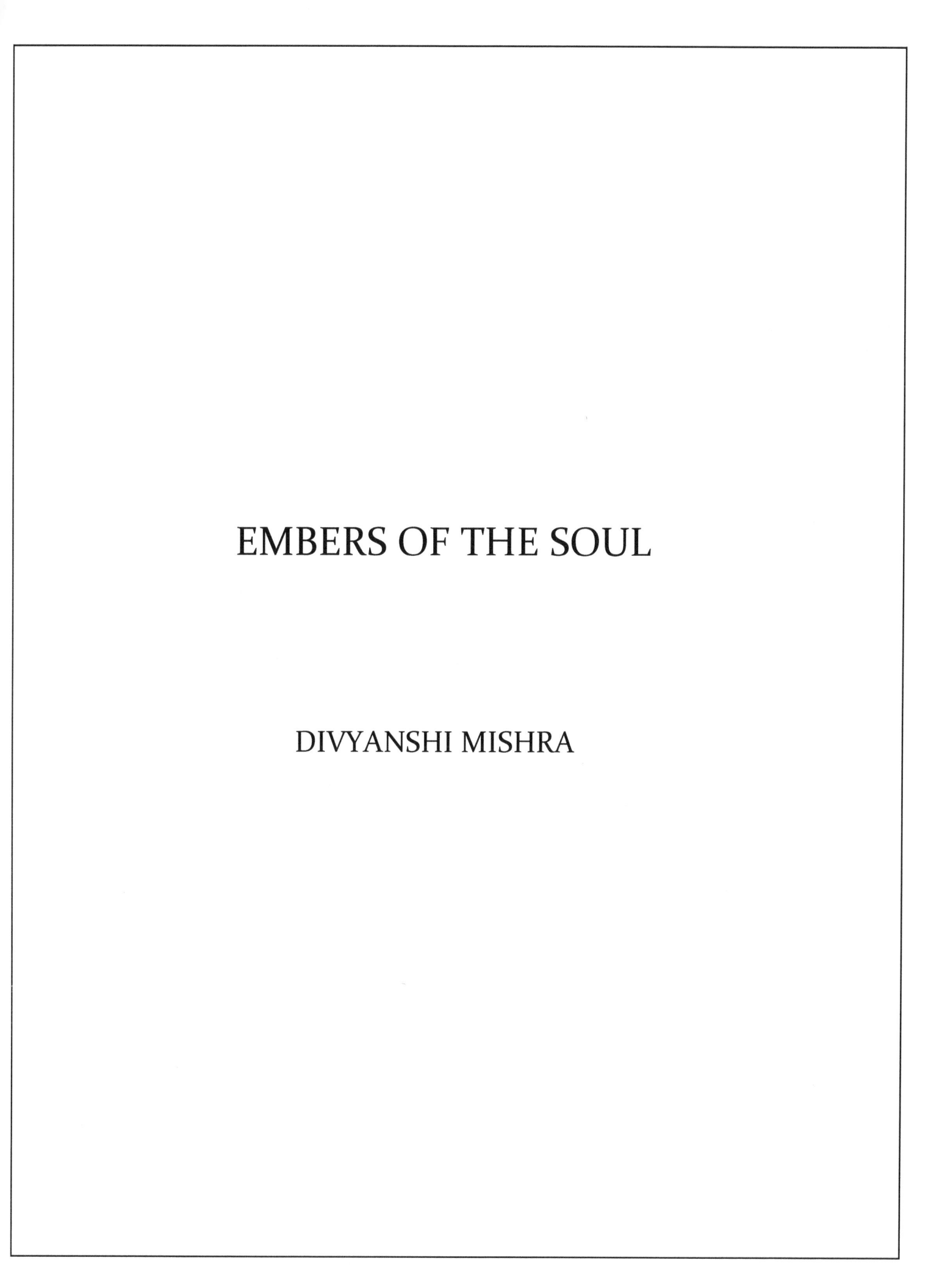

DIVYANSHI MISHRA

Copyright © 2024 Divyanshi Mishra
All rights reserved.
ISBN :
Gmail – divyanshixavier2008@gmail.com
YouTube - divyanshi_mishra01
Illustrations by - ig: @sharmachad7

For my mom and dad,

My heart is a flower at your feet.
Thankyou for being that unwavering constant supporters, anyone could
ask for. I hope you're feeling proud of me.
Yes! that's the only motto of my life.
(To give you both all the happiness with all the possibilities I could reach to,
because parents like you deserve the entire universe.)

I love you!

Dear reader,

My warmest greetings with my warmest hugs to

you!

(for you deserve it wholly and soully.)

I hope you really enjoy the time feeling and reading those wrapped emotions which I weaved here into verses, in this book 'EMBERS OF THE SOUL'. I'm sure you would relate some of my poems with you because it's more or less inspired by the obstacles or basically those harsh, thick conflicts which we generally faces at this point of time in our life.

You'll like it, hopefully.

Have a good time!

I wish you lots of

happiness.

(for it matters to me a lot

.)

Acknowledgement

To be honest, my journey into poetry began very unexpectedly during one random quiet afternoon, when I was a 9 grader. I was sitting on my bedroom floor, surrounded by stacks of books, when I stumbled upon various parts of trilogies by [Amish Tripathi sir, my all time favourite and also my biggest source of inspiration and motivation, at the same time.]

As I read his words, I felt an undeniable connection to the emotions he conveyed. I was captivated by the way he could transform feelings into beautifully woven verses. Inspired, I picked up a notebook and began to write my own thoughts and experiences.

At first, it was a way to express my feelings during difficult times, a safe space where I could pour my heart onto a page.

Each poem became a little piece of me, reflecting my own joys, my own sorrows, and everything in between.

Over the years, writing poetry became more than just a pastime; it grew into a passion, and my favorite habit which I cherish the most. I began to share my work with my friends, my teachers and my family of course, who encouraged me to keep writing. Their support ignited a fire within me, pushing me to explore new themes and styles, and then gradually with time I realized that poetry became my refuge, a way to navigate my life's ups and downs.

First and foremost, I thank my parents for their unconditional love and encouragement at every step. Your belief in me has been my greatest source of strength at all times no matter what.

To my teachers, Thank you so much for being so kind, generous and sweet to me, you all made my school days worth it and I'll be forever grateful for this. Thank you for believing in my works, and providing me with ample of opportunities all the time, Thank you for always making me realize of the potential I hold.

To my friends, thank you for your support and for always being my first audience. Your corrections when I went wrong, and your motivation, your claps, and your appreciations at the same time has enriched my work immeasurably.

Last but never the least,

Thank you my dear readers for giving me a read.

Once again, I owe a debt of gratitude to everyone who has supported me, inspired me to share my voice with the world.

Now, as I present this collection of my poems, I am immensely grateful for the journey that has brought me here.

I know it's of course a long way to go before I call myself a poetess but then, presenting this book has given me a strongest sensation to my sensitive heart of starting something like a journey, and

I'm in love with this process.

Significance of the title

'EMBERS' are basically the smoldering parts of a fire that can reignite if more fuel or oxygen is added, which is why they're often used to restart fires. Symbolically, they represent something that, while diminished, still has potential (just like you), energy, or life left in it.

So, basically the title of my book "EMBERS OF THE SOUL" symbolizes the quiet, enduring aspects of our inner self—those parts of our soul that continue to glow even after life's fiercest challenges or most transformative experiences.

Much like the embers of a fire, which hold heat and potential even after the flames have died down, the embers of the soul represent the resilience, lingering passions, and extinguished hope that remain within us, even when life seems difficult or our energy feels depleted.

(I hope you liked the title).

CONTENT

NO.	Poems	pages
1	Catalyst of my gloomy life	1
2	Supporters is all we need	2
3	My isolated soul	3
4	Oh! My motivating haters	4
5	Confidence that lies	5
6	Wall flower	6
7	My sibling ,my love	7
8	Tick Tick Tock, Oh! my clock	8
9	My birthday	9
10	My childhood days	10
11	Middle class family	11
12	My soul full with spirituality	12
13	Star in the sky	13
14	Soul	14
15	Youth: The beacon of Hope	15
16	Who says man don't cry?	16
17	Embrace of darkness	17
18	That beautiful azure	18
19	My mom, my lady	19
20	Veil of night	20
21	Hope	21
22	Oh! my dear banana tree	22
23	My long distanced comrade	23
24	Dance like you alike	24
25	Life	25
26	My last breathe	26
27	My spiritual soul	27
28		28
29	I reclaim my voice	29
30	The toughest goodbye	30

31	You lost me, I clapped	31
32	I miss her	32
33	My lost comrade	33
34	Goodbye	34
35	This is way I love nights.	35
36	Trust	36
37	She	37
38	Rose in my garden	38
39	Precious times together	39
40	My precious necklace	40
41	Home	41
42	Tears	42
43	Zoo	43
44	DIAMONDS, For free	44
45	I love to dance	46
46	Days in summer	47
47	River, the source of my peace	48
48	Doorbell	49
49	Oh! Sweet little bird.	50
50	Friends of ten	51
51	My Brother, my life	52
52	My lost teddy	53
53	My shattered heart	55
54	Cries are my forever friends	56
55	Rain	57
56	Curiosity that lies	58
57	Young princess in her	59
58	Halloween week	60
59	A Beacon of light	61
60	Am I really unlucky?	63
61	That obsessed me	64
62	Betrayal	65
63	It made me strong	66
64	Counting colors	67
65	Why, I became a selectovert?	68
66	Unity	69
67	The bridge I couldn't remake	70

68	Love that's lost	71
69	My heart aches harder	72
70	The Papaya tree	73
71	VANADIUM in person	74
72	"The beautiful bestowal	75
73	I wish my heart could speak	76
74	Excuses	77
75	Grade X	78
76	MY LOVE, one-way	80
77	My love for poetry	81
78	The color which I like	82
79	Oh love!, my love	83
80	My pet, my parrot, my love	84
81	My pet, my blacky	85
82	Oh! my grandma	86
83	My dad, My superhero	87
84	Oh!, my beloved	88
85	The mirror that speaks	89
86	Oh!, my broken heart	90
87	Shadows	91
88	Fear!	92
89	Searching for peace	93
90	Those stars of hope	94
91	My love for journalism	95
92	Truss you hair tight	96
93	Saw grandpa on the chair	97
94	Date	98
95	Curse not murphy	99
96	Constant	100
97	Friendship	102
98	That desperate flame inside	103
99	My swaddled freedom	104
100	Fear of success, and A hope to light	105
101	Promises which never turned true	106
102	The weight of should	107
103	This is why I like Darkness	108
104	My precious gems, my buddies	109

105	A winner in me	110
106	Divine power knot that ties me	111
107	Gregarious	112
108	My soft corner, my bedroom	113
109	She, A dreamer, A winner	114
110	My school crush	115
111	My wings	116
112	Dreams	117

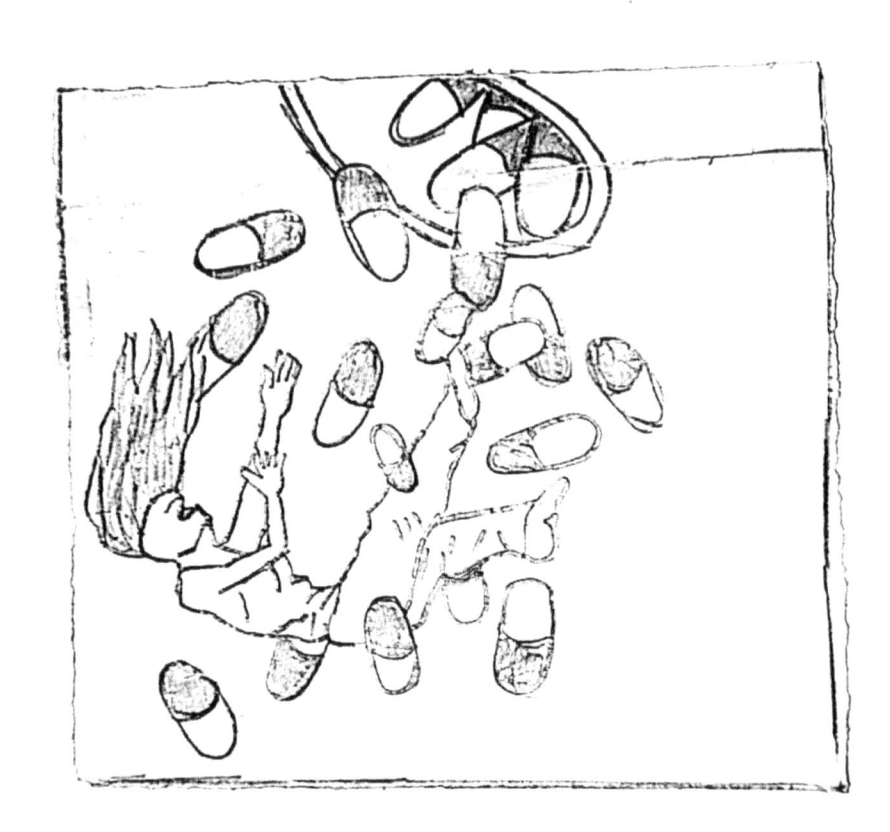

Catalyst of my gloomy life

In the quiet corners of my restless days,

You spark the fire,

ignite the blaze.

when shadows loom heavy and paths seem unclear,

Your voice cuts through doubt, your vision draws near.

You see the potential in me that who I am,

guiding me gently, like a bright guiding star.

With every challenge that rises to meet,

You stand there beside me, unwavering, sweet.

You challenge my limits, expand my horizons,

with courage and kindness,

you help me rise on.

So, here's to the motivators of my life, steadfast and true,

The ones who believe,

who see me anew.

May your light keep on shining,

because in your embrace,

I find strength and delight.

Supporters is all we need

Through trials and triumphs, you cheer and you guide,
A beacon of hope,
A warm, constant tide.

In the game of life,

when the stakes feel high,

You are the wind beneath our wings, WE FLY!

each word you utter,

A thread of pure gold,

weaving strength into hearts that once felt cold.

Through laughter and tears, through losses and wins,
Your unwavering support is where strength begins.
So, here's to the ones who believe in our dreams,
The loyal supporters,
The silent moonbeams.

May we honor your love with each step that we take, because in every endeavor,
it's you who we stake.

My isolated soul

The world outside feels sharp, too loud,
So, I drift away, wrapped up in a cloud.

It's not that I don't long for light,
But peace, I find, in endless night.
The noise of life, it presses near,
So, I retreat, escape my fear.
I build walls, brick by brick,
To shield my soul, to feel less sick.

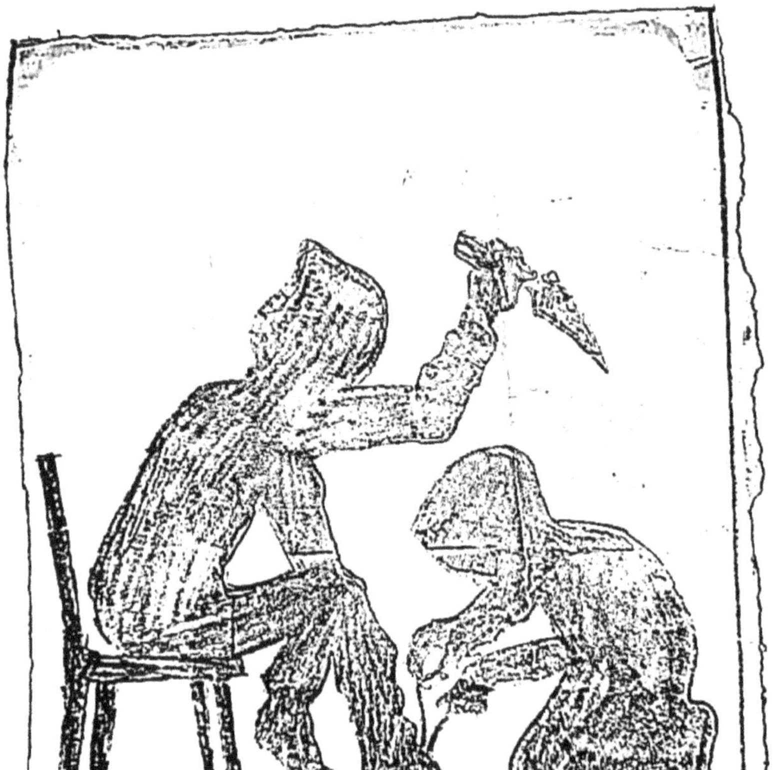

Oh! my motivating haters.

You point out my flaws,
you mock and you sneer,
But your bitter words only sharpen my cheer.
For every cruel comment,
I rise even higher,

fuelling my passion,

IGNITING MY FIRE!

You underestimate the strength in my heart,

Assuming your words could tear me apart.

but like a tough seed that pushes through stone,

I flourish in soil that you thought was alone.

Your envy, a mirror reflecting your fear,

while I grow unbound,

My vision is clear.

with every dismissal,

I gather my might,

turning your darkness into my light.

So, seriously thank you for showing me who I can be,

A warrior of dreams, fierce and free.

Your hate is a lesson, a

step on my way,

because I'll thrive in the sunshine of a brighter day.

Confidence

With every step, a heartbeat strong,

A voice that knows it can't be wrong.

It stands tall like the mighty oak,

unyielding in the words it spoke.

through storms and trials,

It won't bend,

Then I starts thinking I'm a trusted friend.

With eyes ablaze and purpose bright,

It dances boldly in the light.

For confidence is not mere pride,

But the courage found when

fears subside.

So, let it rise, this flame within,   A journey bold,

where dreams begin.

with every challenge,

it will grow.

A true feeling to the strength I know!

Wall flower

In quiet corners, soft and still,

A life is lived with thoughtful will.

They find their peace in moments small,

The hush of rain, the night's cool call.

The world within, a sacred space,

where dreams and thoughts weave, slow in grace.

Though they may hide from crowds and noise,

Their heart is full, their mind enjoys.

because in the calm, they see the light,

An introvert's world, serene and bright!

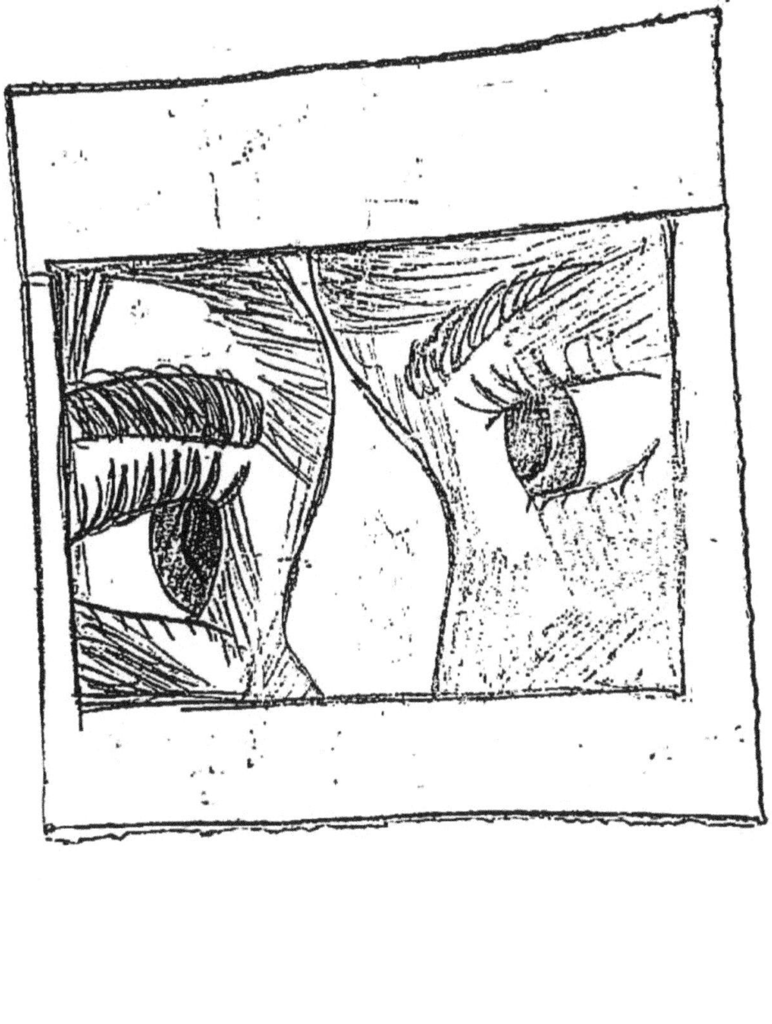

My sibling, my love

In the heart of every home, they grow,

Side by side, through highs and low.

Shared laughter, shared tears,

bound by love through all the years.

A mirror, a shadow, a friend so near,

Through every joy, through every fear.

They fight, they mend, they laugh again,

In each other's heart, they remain.

Though paths may part, and time may drift,

The bond of siblings is a timeless gift.

In every hug, in every glance,

They find in each other a second chance.

A love unspoken, but always known,

In a sibling's heart, you're never alone.

I love you!

Tick! Tick! Tock!, oh! my clock

Tick! tock! the clock does chime,

blubbering secrets of passing time.

moments slip through fingers tight,

morning fades into the night.

Each second, a gentle sigh,

carrying dreams, letting them fly.

hours dance with fleeting grace,

Leaving footprints we cannot trace.

Silent witness to joy and pain, It never stops, though we remain.
Measuring love, loss, and hope,

A timeless rhythm helps us cope.

Though its hands may never slow,
In its beat, we learn and grow.

The clock ticks on, a steady guide,

Through life's vast and changing tide.

My birthday

Another year, a page that turns,

A candle flickers, soft and burns.

The echoes of the past we hear,

Both joy and sorrow, near and dear.

A journey marked by steps so small,

By dreams that rise, by fears that fall.

With every tear and every smile,

We've walked this path, mile by mile.

But today's not just about the years,

Or all the triumphs, all the tears.

It's celebration, pure and bright,

 of moments bathed in love and light.

Now grown, but still I hold it near,
A treasure chest of joy and cheer.
For in my heart, that child remains,
Untouched by time, untouched by change.

(Just like me,
do you also miss your childhood,
 "ofcourse yes!"
 would be your answer,
I know.)

Middle class family

With worn-out shoes and hopes held high,

We navigate life, just you and I.

From schoolyard dreams to workday strife,

In the journey of living, we weave our life.

Through the hustle and bustle,

the chaos we find,

In the midst of the noise, our hearts are aligned.

Each
struggle we face, every challenge we meet,
Is woven with love, making our lives complete.

Though our means may be humble,

Our spirits soar high, with roots deeply planted,

we reach for the sky.

because in love's sweet embrace,

we find strength anew, In a

middle-class life,

our dreams will come true. (-Amen!)

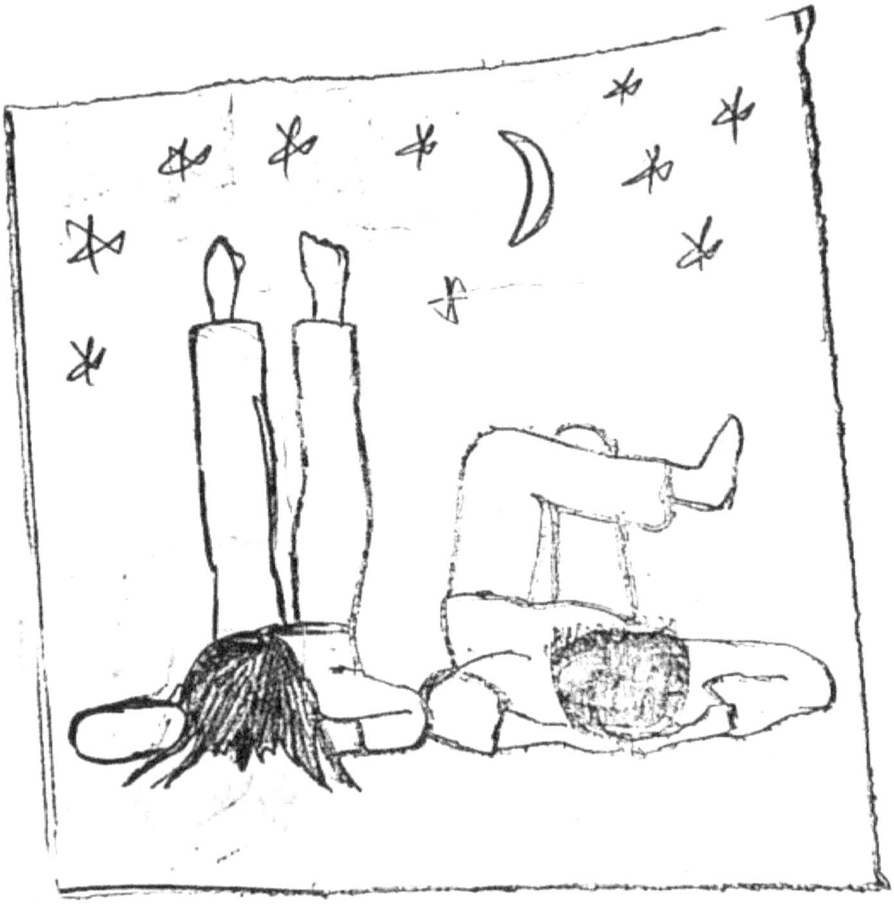

Who says men don't cry?

Who says men don't cry,
when the heart feels the ache inside?
Tears fall like silent rain, Washing away unspoken pain.

Strength is not in holding back, But in the courage to face the cracks.
So, let the tears fall from your eye-
Who says men don't cry?

Embrace of Darkness

In shadows deep,
the night does creep,
A silent veil where
secrets sleep.
But in the dark,
A spark may rise,
A hidden light beneath closed eyes.

That beautiful azure

The azure unfurls in hues of blue,
with clouds that dance in light's soft hue.
A canvas wide, both vast and high,
A silent wonder, the endless sky.
At dawn it glows, at dusk it sighs,
A world of beauty in our eyes. Beneath its gaze, we dream and fly,
Lost in the magic of the sky.

My mom, my lady

Your gentle hands,
Your endless care,
A love so pure, beyond compare.
In every smile and every tear, You've held me close, kept me near.

Through all the storms,
You've been my guide,
A light that shines from deep inside.
No words enough, no gift too grand,
To thank you, Mom,
for who I am.

(You're the only person in this world whom I love the most!)

Veil of night

Darkness falls like a whispered breath,
Silencing the world, in quiet death.
It wraps the earth in a cold embrace,
hiding all in its shadowed grace.

Yet in the black, there's more to see,
A realm where dreams roam wild and free.
The stars are lost, but hope remains,
A flicker where the silence reigns.

For darkness is not just an end,
But where the broken start to mend.
In its stillness, hearts can grow,
 Awaiting dawn's gentle glow.

Hope

When the world says "no," and paths seem blocked,
When every door feels tightly locked,
Hold tight to hope, and never bend,
And you know why?
Just because every storm will someday end.

You carry a spark, an unyielding flame,
That no defeat can ever claim. Through trials fierce and moments grim,
Your spirit's song will never dim.

So march ahead, despite the strain,
Through every loss,
through every pain.
because in your soul, a truth remains,
You are the light that breaks the chains.

(Let's hope for the best, till the last!)

Oh, my dear banana tree

Tall and gentle,
You sway with grace,
rooted strong in its sacred place.
leaves like fans in the summer breeze,
A quiet strength among the trees.

Through storm and sun,
it stands so true,
with fruit that thrives, and life anew.
The banana tree, both soft and strong,
A symbol of endurance all along.

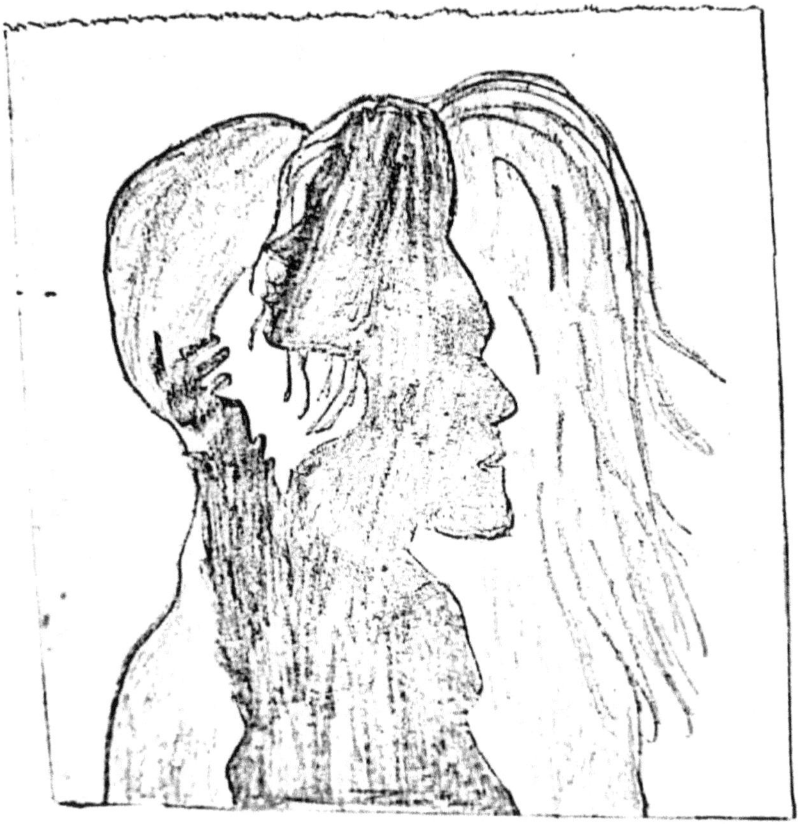

My long distanced comrade

Distance and time has made me stronger,
My love for you will last, that much longer.
There's not even a single night when I don't think of you,
moon afar has also started understanding my real fondness for you!
don't know why this distance is tearing us apart
approximating that,
This span is not aware of our love.
Don't know how to be thankful to you!
A bit shy to say that
"I love you!"
Missing those abusive talks and of course our fights,
How can I forget those of chats late nights,
This shattered lone heart needs you badly!
Come and hug me, more way tightly.
The one who hated phone calls has started loving and making it a daily routine,
You are my forever unpaid therapist
who listens to all my boring and nonsense history.
and also helps me in chemistry and other studies.
Thought this poem would end in lines six or eight,
but it's forcing me to write more about you because
You're my true beloved comrade,
whom I do miss a lot and loves more than anybody knows
No one can ever take your place or break this bond
for you are my precious gem who even taught me how to cross the road.

(I hope u miss me and love me the same way I do!)

Dance, how you wish alike

The days blend together,
a blur in our sight,
chasing the shadows that dance in the light.
But pause for a moment, breathe deep, take a glance,
In the chaos of busy,
Don't forget to dance.

Life

Dance through the storms,
and sing through the pain,
For each trial endured,
There's wisdom to gain.

In the dance of existence,
with all of its strife,
we discover the beauty,
the miracle of life!

 (Life is full of ups and downs,
thicks and thins but I truly wish,
that your life may fill with sunflowers
and more beautiful people like you.)

My last breathe

As I exhale,
I feel the release,
A gentle surrender,
A heart filled with peace. Though I leave behind the skin and bone,
In spirit, I soar, forever not alone.

So, remember
me not in sorrow or pain,
but in love's sweet refrain,
like soft summer rain.
In every heartbeat, in every sigh,
I live on in the love that will never die.

My spiritual soul

In the hush of dawn,
where shadows retreat,
A whisper stirs softly, a pulse,
A heartbeat.
The world awakens, draped in gold light,
And in that still moment,
The spirit takes flight.

Beyond the confines of flesh and of bone,
Lies a realm of existence,
both vast and unknown.
In the breath of the trees,
In the dance of the sea,
A sacred connection,
The essence of me.

The mountains stand tall, guardians of time,
Echoing secrets in rhythm and rhyme.
with each rustling leaf, a story is told,
of journeys untraveled, of spirits so bold.

In silence,
I wander through valleys of grace,
where love is the compass, and truth leaves its trace.

The cosmos above in its infinite sprawl,
reminds me of oneness,
The answer to all.

In the laughter of children, in tears that we shed,
In moments of stillness,
where fears are allayed.
I find the divine in the mundane and small,
In the mosaic woven,
I see I'm a part of it all.

So I surrender my heart to the flow of the day,
Trusting the journey,
come what may.
because in the depths of my soul, I finally see.
The sacredness of life an eternal decree.

(Believing in god has made me what I'm today,
 Trust in God, he will take you to the places
and give you happiness more than you deserve.)

I reclaim my voice

With each step I take,
I reclaim my voice,
In the silence of fear,
I make my own choice.
No longer confined by the whispers of shame,
I rise from the ashes,
I'm reclaiming my name.
with the heart of a warrior,
I stand on my own,
In the pride of my journey,
I've fully grown.
because within every woman, a lioness dwells,
with stories of strength that her spirit compels.
with grace in my heart and strength in my stride,
I rise like the dawn,
with the lioness inside!

The toughest goodbye

Now as I breathe my final sigh, I'll carry your love as I say goodbye.
Each whispered word, a tender thread,
woven in the words we've said.

So hold my hand, don't be afraid,
because in this journey,
Love won't fade.
In the garden of memories,
I'll be near, In every heartbeat, I'll always be here.

(I know it's tough, but completely fine!)

You lost me, I clapped

Every touch was a promise, every glance a vow,
but time has a way of changing the how.
You're a fleeting thought,
A bittersweet dream,
yet love is a gentle current continues to stream.

I miss her

We wandered through days, side by side,

In the warmth of your smile,
I would confide.
Through joys and sorrows,
We faced the storm,
In your presence,
I always felt warm.

But time has a way of pulling apart,
Distance and silence can break the heart.
I search for your laughter in the echoes of now,
seriously wondering how life has led us to how.

The memories linger like soft, fading light,
In quiet reflections of long, lonely nights.
I hold onto moments when we were so free,
A bond unbroken, in spirit, you're with me!

Though you may wander on paths unknown,
In the garden of my heart,
your seeds are sown.
I cherish our friendship, though we are apart,

For you'll always remain a piece of my heart.
 So, here's to the days when we danced in the sun,
To the laughter and love,
Our hearts became one.
In every memory, you'll never fade away,
My lost friend, forever, come what may.

My lost comrade

Once we laughed under skies so blue,
Every moment shared felt so true.
with whispers of dreams and secrets we told,
A friendship forged,
more precious than gold.

I truly miss you,

hope we both meet one day

maybe randomly in the busy roads of parallel universe,

somewhere, someday.

Goodbye

So here in this silence,
I'll hold you close,
In the depth of my heart, you're the one I love most. Though distance may part us, and life may divide,
The whispers of the heart will always abide.
Your smile was a sunrise,
my favorite view,
Now clouds cloak the memories I once knew.
I search for the fragments of all that we were,
In the silence between us,
my heart starts to stir.
I reach for your hand,
but you're nowhere near,
Just whispers of echoes that I long to hear.
Yet, even in absence,
your spirit remains,
A bittersweet melody that softly sustains.
You were the sun in my stormiest skies,
A comforting presence, where truth never lies.
But time slipped away,
like sand through my hands, Leaving me lost in unfamiliar lands.
The weight of goodbye lingers heavy and cold,
A chapter unfinished, a story untold.
Yet, in my heart, your memory
stays bright,

A guiding star in the depths of the night.

This is why I love nights

The moon hangs low,
a silvery guide,
casting soft shadows where wishes reside.
with each breath of night,
the worries unwind,
In the stillness,
I find peace of mind.
In the quietest hours,
where hearts can confide,
We share our hopes,
with nothing to hide.
A canvas of dreams, so vivid and pure.
In the dance of the stars,
I find my delight,
For in the embrace of the night, I feel right.
I lose myself in the magic of dark,
where every heartbeat ignites a spark.

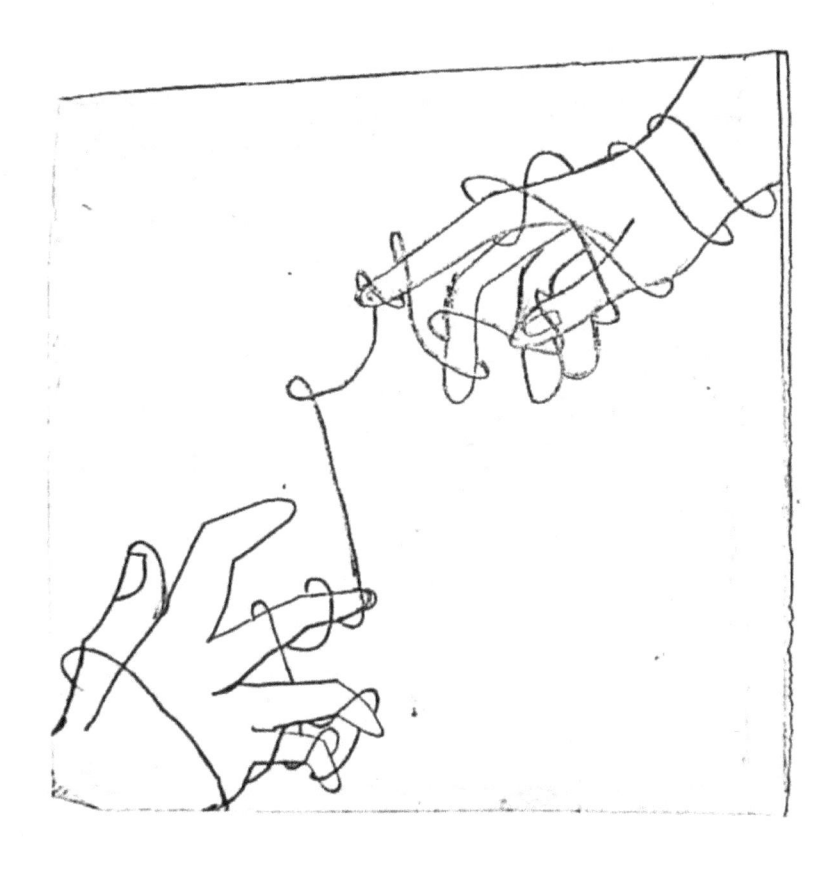

Trust

Like a gentle breeze on a summer's day,
Trust nurtures love in its own tender way.
It's the silence shared in a knowing glance,
The courage to leap, to give love a chance.

In shadows of doubt, it stands like a light,
A beacon that guides us through the darkest of nights.
It blooms in the moments when words fall away,
In the steadfast presence that never will sway.

She

She nurtures the world with her soft, tender touch,
A healer, a dreamer, she gives so much.
her spirit, unyielding, a fire that won't cease,
In the quiet of
darkness, she finds her peace.

Come on princess,
awake! arise!
proliferate your wings
higher

Rose in my garden

In the garden where dreams take flight,
A rose unfolds in the soft morning light.
with petals like velvet, kissed by the dew,
It dances with grace in a world painted new.

Crimson and gold, with shades rich and deep,
Each hue tells a story, a secret to keep.
Its fragrance, a whisper of love in the air,
A symphony blooming, a tender affair.

Thorns guard its beauty, fierce yet refined,
A reminder that softness is often confined.
Yet through every struggle, it stands with pride,
In the face of the storm, it will not hide.

The rose is a symbol of passion and grace,
of moments of joy and the heart's warm embrace.
In gardens of life,
where emotions entwine,
It flourishes brightly, a treasure divine.

So let us admire this wonder so rare,
A rose in full bloom, beyond compare.
For in its delicate charm, we find a sweet truth:
Beauty often flourishes amidst trials of youth.

Precious times together

We've traveled the mountains, sailed the deep sea,
with you, my dear love, I am always free.
In your eyes, I find hope, in your smile, my peace,
with each passing moment, my love will increase.

Time is a river, flowing endlessly wide,
Yet, in your embrace,
I'll forever abide.
with every heartbeat, our stories unfold,
A mosaic woven with threads of pure gold.

My precious necklace!

Upon my neck, it gently lays,
A thread of time through nights and days.
Each bead, each gem, a moment dear,
A silent whisper I hold near.
A gift of love, a bond so true, With every glance,
I think of you.
Your touch, your warmth, forever stays,
In this precious necklace that never sways.
More than jewels, more than chain,
 It holds my heart through joy and pain.
A story woven with love and care,
My precious necklace, always there.

My precious necklace
 with beads so blue
 is as precious
as you are for me.

Home.

Home is where the heart resides,
In quiet rooms and starry skies. Where every corner hums with peace,
and worries seem to find release.
It's the warmth of arms, a gentle hand,
The soil where roots grow strong and grand.
Wherever we wander, wherever we roam,
There's nothing as sweet as coming home.

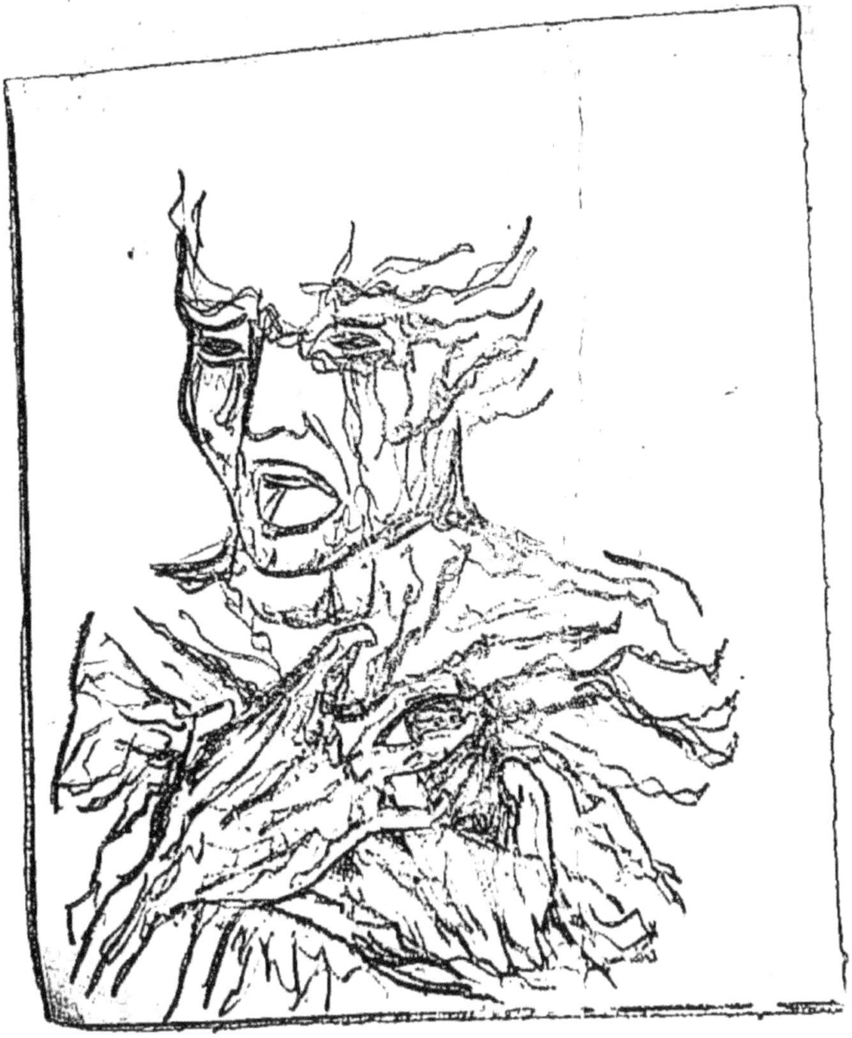

Tears

Tears fall like whispers, soft and slow,
Silent messengers of pain we don't show.
In their shimmer lies a story untold,
of love, of loss, of hearts grown cold.

They trace the path where sorrow's been,
washing the soul, yet never seen.
A fleeting moment, a fragile grace,
that slips like rain upon the face.
Yet, in those tears, there's strength unknown,
A quiet power we call our own. For every drop that falls,
we rise, resilient
beneath the weeping skies.

So let them fall, and let them flow,
For in each tear, we heal, we grow.

Zoo

Step through the gates of a wild, wondrous land,
where creatures from far-off places stand hand in hand.
The roar of the lion, the chatter of birds,
A symphony of nature, no need for words.
beneath the tall trees, the monkeys swing high,
with laughter and mischief, they leap through the sky.
In enclosures of splendor, the elephants sway,
with trunks raised in greeting, they dance through the day. The zebras wear stripes,
A bold black and white,
As they graze on the grass, a magnificent sight.
Giraffes reach for treetops, their necks long and lean, Graceful and gentle, they roam in the green.
The polar bear splashes in cool, sparkling blue,
while the kangaroos hop in their own joyful crew.
each turn in the path, a new wonder unfolds,
As stories of wildlife in whispers are told.
with eyes wide in wonder, we explore every zone,
In this zoo of enchantment, we're never alone.
From the smallest of critters to the grandest of beasts,
Each visit a treasure, where adventure never ceases.
So, come, take a journey through habitats vast,
In the zoo's lively heart,
we find joy that will last.
For here, in this tapestry of life, wild and free,
We celebrate nature's magic, together, you and me.

DIAMONDS, for free!

Family is a bond unspoken,

A thread that weaves through time,

A mosaics of love and life, a rhythm and a rhyme.

It's more than blood,

more than name,

more than what we see,

It's the gentle hands that hold us up and set our spirits free. In childhood's laughter, bright and clear, in footsteps soft and small,

Family is the ones who catch us whenever we may fall.. Through scraped-up knees and tear-streaked eyes, they wipe away our pain,

and teach us how to stand again, to rise and try again.

In moments grand or moments small, in joy and grief and strife,

Family's the constant thread that stitches through our life. It's the warmth that fills the quiet nights, the light on darkest days.

The steady beat that guides our feet along life's winding ways.

They're the ones who see us clearly, who know just who we are,

who cheer us on from
sidelines near or watch us from afar.

In every smile and every tear, in every triumph won..
Family is the endless flame that's brighter than the sun. Through seasons shifting, years that pass,
they grow but never leave, In every heart,
they plant a seed, a memory to retrieve.
Though paths may part and roads may wind,
though distance may divide,
The love of family is a flame that burns deep down inside. It's in the stories handed down, in voices that we know,
The echo of our ancestors in the way we laugh and grow.
In every shared embrace, each fight, each healing, each goodbye,
Family's the root beneath our feet, the wings that help us fly. And when the world seems vast and cold, when shadows start to fall, It's family that will guide us home,
the truest home of all.
For in their arms, we find our strength, our shelter from the storm,
In family's love, we're always safe, forever safe and warm.
So, here's to family, fierce and true, the anchor in our sea,

The ones who hold us when we're weak,

who love us endlessly.

For family is the heart of life, the reason that we grow

A gift that keeps on giving, as the years and rivers flow.

I love to Dance

In the quiet of the night,
or the heat of the day,
Dance is the language the body must say.
with a spin and a step, a rise and a fall,
Dance is the heartbeat, the pulse of it all.
It's the music that flows through veins like a stream, The rhythm that
wakes us from slumber or dream.
Each movement a story, each gesture a word,
In the silence of motion, the soul is heard.
with feet to the ground and arms to the sky,
We dance out our worries, I let my heart fly.
In sway or in leap, in turns sharp or smooth,
There's magic in movement, there's power to soothe.
For dance is a freedom no walls can contain,
A release of the body, an end to the strain.
It whispers of joy, it shouts through the air,
A moment of truth, of beauty laid bare.
whether alone in the dark or with others in light,
Dance is a language that transcends the night.
It binds us together, it breaks us apart,
It's the rhythm of living, the song of the heart.
So let yourself move, let your body be free,
Dance is the story you're meant to decree.

In the sway of your hips, in the grace of your hands,
You'll find yourself soaring, no need for commands.
For dance is the soul's way to speak, to be heard,
A poem in motion, more pure than a word.
It lives in the body, it breathes in the air-
When you dance, you become the song that you wear.

Days in summer

In the golden glow of summer's light,
Fields of green bask in the warmth so bright.
with every breeze, the world comes alive,
nature's canvas, where joy can thrive.
The sun paints the sky in hues of blue,
As laughter and whispers float softly through.
Children chase dreams in the heat of the day,
while fireflies dance as the twilight holds sway.
The scent of blossoms, sweet and pure,
A symphony of life, we can't ignore.
Long, lazy evenings wrapped in twilight's embrace,
Every moment a treasure, each smile a trace.
As waves kiss the shore and the world feels wide,
In summer's embrace, there's no need to hide.
Let's gather these memories, let them ignite,
because in summer's warmth, our hearts take flight.

River, my source of peace

Through valleys and meadows, the river flows wide,
A ribbon of silver, with secrets inside.
It dances through sunlight, it glimmers and shines,
A storyteller weaving through nature's designs.
gentle ripples murmur, as stones softly sigh,
reflecting the skies and the clouds drifting by.
The banks wear a mosaic,
lush greens and bright hues, Where willows lean down, and the morning dew blues.
fish dart in the shadows, a flicker of gold,
while dragonflies hover, their beauty unfolds.
The laughter of children, as they splash in the stream, Echoes of joy, like a sweet, fleeting dream.
In the hush of the twilight, when the sun starts to dip,
The river sings softly, a tender, sweet lip.
Moonlight will cradle its waters so deep,
As crickets and frogs join the night in their leap.
each twist and each turn tells a story of time.
of journeys and seasons, of reason and rhyme.
In the heart of the river, where life ebbs and flows,
I find my own paths in the currents it knows.
So come, you too come,
sit beside it, let your worries unwind,
In the whispers of water,
A solace you'll find.
For the river's embrace is a timeless retreat,
A haven of peace where our spirits are sweet.

Doorbell

At the quiet hour, when shadows blend,
A gentle chime
beckons,
a trusted friend.
echoes of laughter and stories unfold,
Each ring of the doorbell,
A promise retold.
with each eager buzz, the world draws near,
Connecting the heartbeats, dispelling the fear.
A visitor's presence, a moment to share,
In the warmth of the doorway, love lingers in air.
So ring, little doorbell,
with your sweet sound,
For within these four walls, joy knows no bounds.
Let the laughter and memories, like
petals, unfurl,

In the mosaic woven by each friendly swirl.

Oh! sweet little bird

In the early light,
As dawn breaks anew,
A symphony rises,
fresh as the dew.
The birds lift their voices,
A sweet serenade,
A chorus of chirping in the sunlit glade.
 With notes that flutter like leaves in the breeze,
They dance on the air, putting hearts at ease.
Each trill tells a story, each whistle a song,
A melody weaving where all souls belong.
 From the robin's rich tones to the sparrow's soft call,
Their harmonies mingle, enchanting us all.
In the branches above,
where the wild blossoms sway,
The birds sing their secrets, welcoming day.
 So pause for a moment,
let the music unfold,
In the chirping of birds, there's a magic untold.
A reminder of beauty in life's simple joys,
In the morning's embrace, nature's purest voice.

Friends of Ten

In the halls of memories, we carved our names,
In laughter and whispers, in joys and games.
From morning bell chimes to the noon dismissal,
we wove a tapestries of stories to tell.
with backpacks and dreams, we faced every test,
side by side through the challenges,
we gave it our best.
Late-night study sessions, secrets to share,
building a bond that's
incredibly rare.
From shared glances in class to inside jokes,
every moment together, through laughter we spoke. The crushes we
giggled about, the dreams that we chased, Each memory a treasure,
not one we'll waste.
Though paths may diverge, and time may unfold,
The friendships we nurtured are treasures of gold.
In every reunion, in each heartfelt call,
The spirit of ten will forever stand tall.
So, here's to the
laughter, the tears, and the fun,
To friendships that blossom, two hearts becoming one.
In the book of our lives, you're the brightest of themes,
My friends from tenth grade, you'll forever be dreams.
My dear friends of Ten, You guys were the best of friends anyone could ask for, I know we are all seperated now but will never be seperated by heart.

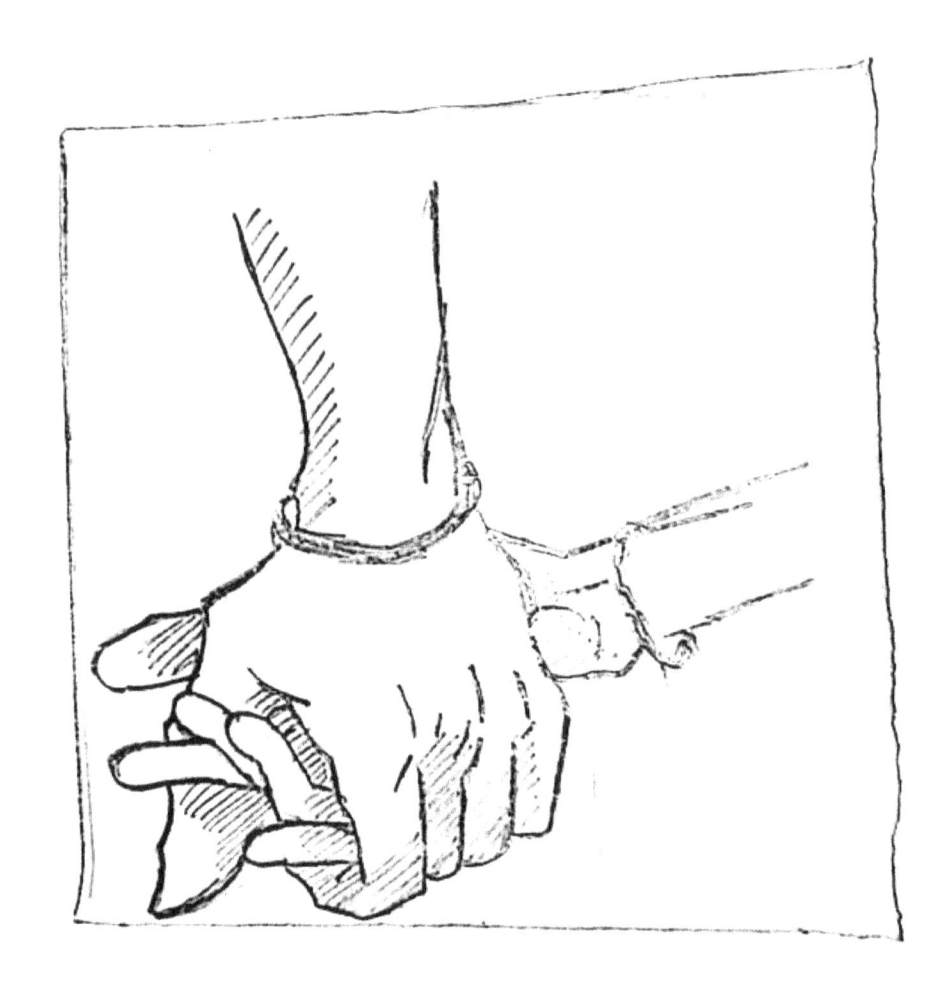

My brother, my life

with every step,

you lead the way,

My brother, my hero,

come what may.

In times of trouble, your voice rings true,

with your steady hand,

I always knew.

You shown me how to stand up tall,

To face the world, to never fall. In every
adventure, in every fight,
You taught me to shine, to seek the light.
Through the years that have flown, like leaves on the
breeze,
Our bond has grown stronger, just like the trees.
So here's to the laughter, the lessons, the fun,
My elder brother, you're second to none.
In the mosaics of life, you're the brightest thread,
with laughter and kindness, you've helped me ahead.

From childhood mischief to dreams we pursue,
In every chapter, I've cherished you!
You've been my protector, my voice of reason,
In every season, you've been my beacon.
with a heart full of wisdom and arms open wide,
You've shown me the beauty of living with pride.
So here's to my brother, my mentor, my friend,
with you by my side,
there's no way to bend.
In the book of my life,
You're the finest part,
Forever and always,
you hold a place in my heart.

My Lost Teddy

In shadows deep,
where dreams once spun, There lies a friend,
my cherished one.
with fur so soft,
and button eyes,
A guardian of secrets,
where laughter lies.

Through countless nights, we shared our fears,
In whispered tales and silent tears.
You held my heart in your gentle embrace,
A comfort found in your warm, plush face.

But now you're gone,
oh where could you be?
A wandering soul, lost from me.
Did you roll beneath the bed? Or find a nook where dreams are fed?

I search the corners,
I call your name,
In every room, it feels the same.
The echoes of laughter,
The warmth of your touch,
A world seems colder without you, so much.

Yet in my heart,
you'll always stay,
A timeless bond that won't decay.
For though you're lost,
my dear old friend,
Our love remains, it will not end.

So here's to you, my teddy bear, Wherever you roam,
I'll always care.
In dreams, I'll find you, soft and near,
My lost companion, forever dear.

My shattered heart

In the silence between us,
I hear our souls speak,
A language of love that's tender and meek.
with every heartbeat,
A promise is made,
In the garden of time,
Our love won't fade.

So let us treasure each moment we share,
In the warmth of your presence, I find my prayer.
For in your embrace,
I have found my way,
Together forever, come what may.

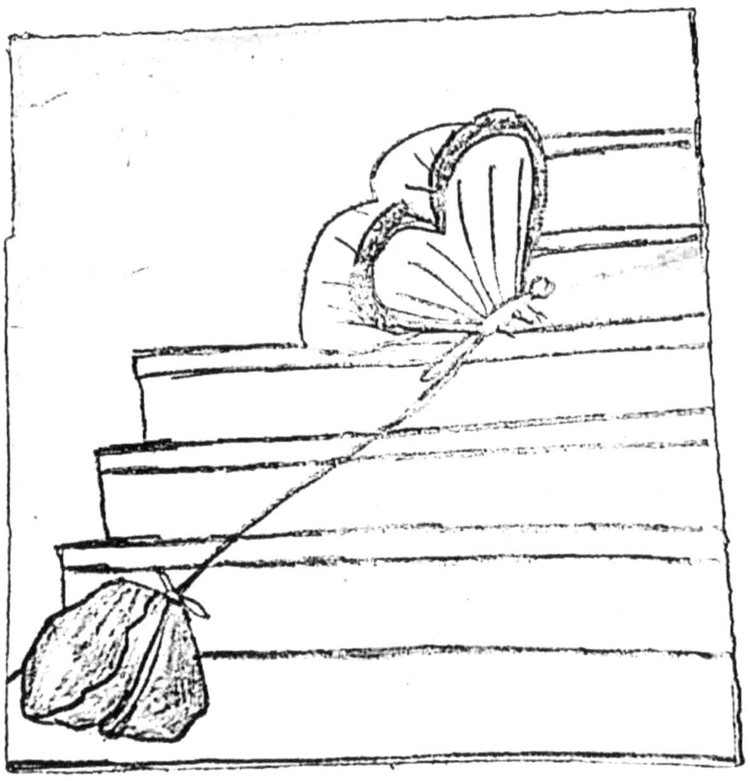

Cries are my forever friends.

In the quiet corners where shadows reside,

My tears become whispers, no longer I hide.

Each drop that falls tells a story untold,

A mosaic woven with threads of pure gold.

They come like a river, unbidden and wild,
A symphony echoing the heart of a child.
In moments of sorrow, they flow with such grace,
A cleansing reminder of this human race.

Also, cries are my friends in the darkest of nights,
They cradle my heart with their gentle insights.
In their soft embrace,
I find solace and strength,
They give voice to feelings, a measure of length.

For in every sob lies a truth we must face,
A journey of healing, a sacred space.
They lift the burdens too heavy to bear,
A testament to love, to loss, and despair.

Through the laughter and joy,
they sometimes appear,
A release of the weight,
A cathartic cheer.
In the dance of emotion,
They twirl and they spin,
reminding me always
that it's okay to begin.
 So I welcome my cries,
These friends of the heart,
For in their raw honesty, healing can start.
With each tear that glistens,
I learn to let go,
Embracing the beauty in all that I know

Rain

Raindrops cascade,
A soft lullaby,
Each one a whisper, a gentle sigh.
we wander through storms, unafraid to get wet,
In the heart of the downpour, our love is our bet.

With each splash and giggle, the world fades away,
You and I are forever in this rainy ballet.
So let the clouds gather, let the thunder call,
In the embrace of the rain, we will conquer it all.

Curiosity

A flicker in the mind's deep well,
where questions rise and answers dwell.
A restless spark that stirs the soul,
Curiosity makes me whole.

It wanders far, it dives in deep,
Unveiling truths the world might keep.
It dares to ask, it seeks to find,
 The hidden paths of heart and mind.

Through every door it opens wide,
new worlds await on the other side.
Curiosity, forever free,
Unlocks the vast infinity.

Young princess in her

In the heart of a castle,

where dreams softly gleam,

A young princess awakens, wrapped in her dream.

with laughter like sunlight,

she dances on air,

her spirit unbroken,

her joys bold and rare.

With each twirl of her gown, she spins tales of old,
of dragons and heroes, of treasures untold.
She wanders through gardens, where wildflowers bloom, Finding magic in moments, dispelling all gloom.

A crown made of daisies rests lightly on her head,
As she chases the whispers that flutter like thread.
Her heart beats in rhythm with the song of the breeze,
For the world is a canvas,
and she paints it with ease.

In the mirror, she sees not just a young face,
But a queen in the making,
full of hope and grace.
with courage as armor and kindness as sword,
she dreams of a future where love is the lord.

So let the young princess, within all of us, rise,
with the light of her spirit, igniting the skies.
For each of us carries a kingdom so vast,
In the heart of a child, our dreams hold steadfast.

Halloween week

Results may falter,

dream may shake,

but in setbacks, new path we make

those palpitating fingers, and face dumb and scared,

that halloween CISCE website, and toxic relatives out there, those calls, pinged notifications, and texts

That huge mass of hesitating humans,

my shattered heart and stiffy soul,

Those high expectations and hopes!!!

Nights of struggles and hardwork,

But then looking at the azure, reminds me of the sunset, Remind me that endings are beautiful but,

beginnings turns out to be more beautiful,

I realised past can't be made,

I realised past are not meant to be regretted,

I realised, present can be made better,

no use of thinking about,
something that never can be refreshed.

why to lose hope when we are more way stronger,
Accept this fact that the single sheet can't decide your future Embrace the lessons,
Failure brings, because you know na?
From the ashes, success springs!!
In the society of the demotivations, stand chill and tall
let courage be your constant call through various tries and fears
Out there you will find your way,
with every step,
A brighter day.

A BEACON OF LIGHT

In every word, in every smile,

YOU have walked with us in each challenging mile!

with open minds and open hearts,

You have given us our brightest starts.

currently in standard 11th,

but how can I forget those days of 10th!

where we prepared to part our ways,

We carried forth your brightest rays!

with gratitude and deep respect, because.

we got the teachers we will never forget!

Not just the lectures and lessons,

but also those moral sessions, have shaped me,

shaped us and made us whole. we came completely rusted but you electroplated us,
were like skeletal equations but you balanced us.
with x's and y's equations galore,
you have shown us maths is never a bore.

with every lesson, a new place is found, broadening horizons turning it around,

A geography teacher,

a true explorer at heart,

inspiring students to chart their own part!

from Ruskin Bond to Shakespeare, MOV to Macbeth, essays to proposals,

You have made us love literature through and through.

with every lesson, a seed is sown
nurturing curiosity making it grow.

Biology teacher at true work of art,

shaping minds and hearts, our lasting start!

from ancient rome to civil war, you have made the past come alive and bright,

with stories that keep us up all night.

with sports and games the days aren't long,

with every sprint and every play,

you make sure that we are active everyday.

supplies and demands,

oh, what a mix!

You have taught us the tricks of economic kicks!

There lessons on light a shining light, illuminating concepts, banishing night.

They lead the journey through physics deeps.

Debit on the left, credit on the right, balancing sheets till late at night.

With gratitude and love,

from Newton's law to quantum leaps,

with ledgers and journals you navigate,

through numbers you truly captivate!
You have challenged, inspired, and
helped us to see the part of learning and who we can be.
For all of your efforts,
Your time and your care we are ready to face life
because you are there!

we all honour you today!

HAPPY TEACHER'S DAY IN EVERY POSSIBLE WAY

Am I really unlucky?

I see, observe, and explore,
I wonder how people bother and adore me,
I wonder how people love and overcare about me,
but the harsh reality is:
'Just before the very eyes of mine'.
rest of the times;
maybe counted as worse,
or even the worst.
People yells and distrust me, They seriously fake love and care.

They misinterprets,

They misunderstands me,

but I feel proud, because...

I hold within myself, the buckets of pure intentions.

I'm alone even though I show myself 'I have many',

but I am not.

I see, 'I have many' for verbal showoffs,

but in real no one is mine. whom to rely on, whom to trust on,

More or less, everyone is same.

Maybe I am wrong, or I

am puzzled or maybe......

weird at some of the times or

situations.
but I'm true, and just asks for cuddles.
I show, I am cool but then I questions...
oh really? but then I
remembers, I am seriously unlucky, for real.

but then, I just hope,

for everything to get assembled.

That, obsessed me

For in loving myself, I see..
The beauty of authenticity! That self obsession and self confidence which I hold,
Me, myself is beautiful and bold!
with each heartbeat, I affirm, My worthiness,
my right to squirm!
Inspite of these many failures and cries,
I stand tall with the power to heal,
and the strength to shine. letting the winds of doubt blow, I stand firm again,
ready to grow...
Each petal of self doubt I pluck, replacing it with self love's luck...
proliferating my wings higher, So that I can fly higher,
and meet God and thank him for
The biggest supporter and the biggest motivator
he gave!
Yes, that's me and that proud figure I stay,
in the mirrors reflection, I see, The greatest love of all, staring back at me.
And that proud tone of mine which says, I am enough,
I declare with
conviction..
A masterpiece in progress, a beautiful rendition.
In my dumb mind, where doubts and fears meet..
I plant seeds of kindness, tender, and true
nurturing self love in all that I do!

Betrayal

A whispered lie in the quiet night,
Once silver-tongued,
now sharp as knives.
The trust we wove in threads so tight,
Unraveled fast before my eyes.

A glance, a touch, a fleeting grin,
Your mask fell off, the truth seeped in.
The bond we held, a fragile thing,
shattered by deceit within.

You wore the face of someone kind,
but hid the truth you left behind.
The promise broken, heart misplaced,
The bitter taste of trust erased.

But though your darkness left a scar,
I stand and rise, not torn apart. For I will heal, and you will see, The strength that grows inside of me.

How easily it is to break or destroy someone, Isn't it?

It made me strong

And when the storm has passed me by,
I'll stand beneath a clearer sky. For though this journey's tough and long,
It shaped my soul,
it made me strong.

Counting colors

I counted the colours in the sky,
Where dawn kissed night a soft goodbye.
One for the blush of morning's hue,
A pink so fresh, so full, so new.

Two for the gold in the sun's first light,
Spilling warmth,
chasing away the night.
Three for the blue that stretched so far,
Touching the edge of the last faint star.

Four for the green in leaves below,
Whispering secrets in the winds that blow.
Five for the purple, deep and bold,
Of twilight dreams the dusk unfolds.

Six for the red of the setting sun,
A fiery farewell when day is done.
Seven for the black, quiet and still,
That wraps the earth in its peaceful will.

But colours, I find, cannot be named,
For in each breath, they shift and change.
A rainbow hides in every shade,
An endless count that cannot fade.

So I lose my place and start anew,
In the ever-shifting spectrum of you.

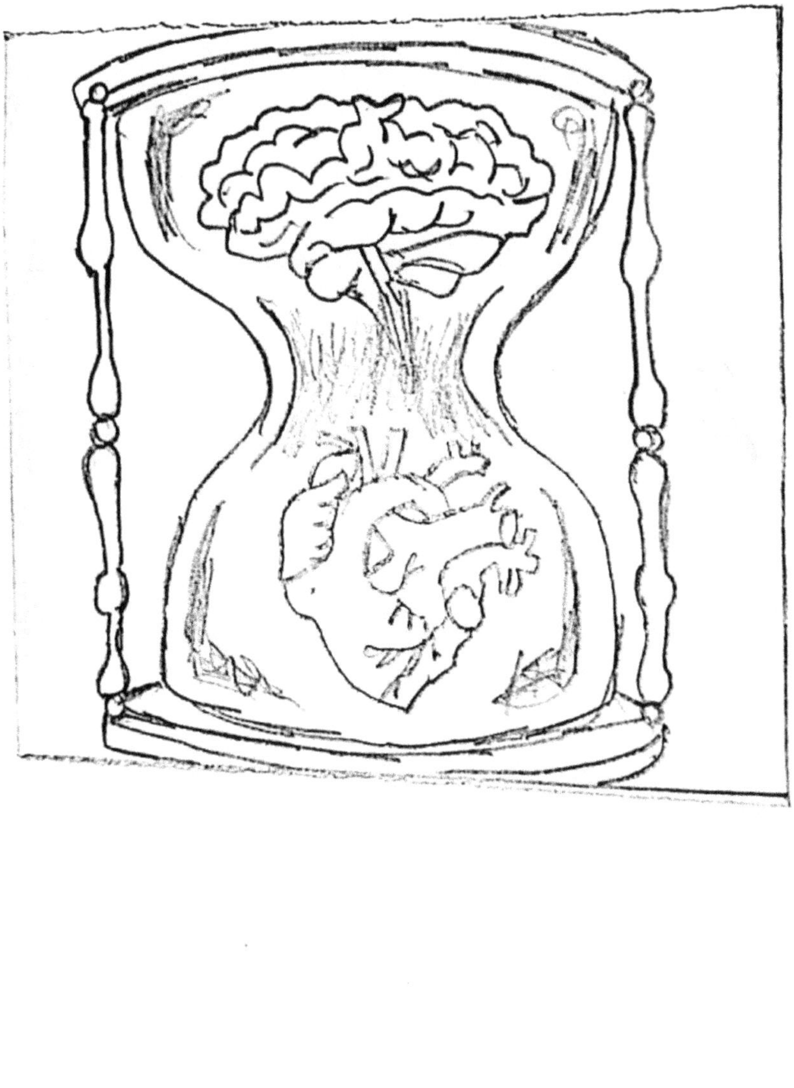

Why, I became a selectovert?

I used to spill my words like rain,
In every crowd, in every lane. Laughter loud,
I'd fill the air,
No room for silence anywhere.

But now I choose my voice with care,
Not every space deserves to share.
Not every ear, nor every eye, Can see the truth behind my sky.

I've learned the art of quiet grace,
of stepping back,
of giving space.
not every spark needs to ignite,
not every battle needs a fight.

I dance between the light and shade,
A presence felt,
but softly made.
A listener now, a subtle part, guarding my mind, protecting my heart.

Why have I started to be this way?
Perhaps,
it's peace I've found in play-
To save my fire for when it's right,
And choose my moments in the light..

For I have learned there's beauty too,
In knowing when to speak,
or not pursue.
A world of balance in between, The seen, unseen, the quiet sheen.

So now I wander, sometimes bold,
Sometimes silent, a story untold.
A selectovert, a shifting tide,
Picking the shores where I'll confide.

Unity

Voices rise like a symphony, Harmonies of hope and dreams,
Different paths converge as one,
A river of strength in shared streams.
Mountains may rise,
storms may rage,
Yet united,
we are never alone,
with hearts intertwined,
we face the tide,
In this vast world,
we've found a home.

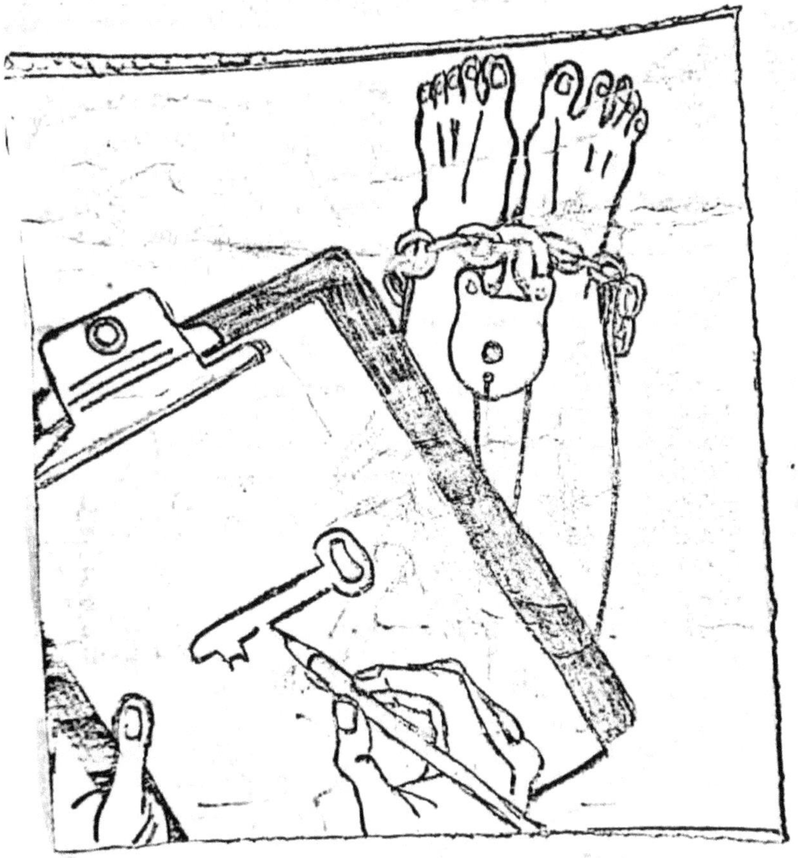

The bridge I couldn't remake

By the colony side,
where we first met, underneath the twilight sky, promises we made,
hand in hand, side by side, truly by heart,
soul and mind.
Hoped for a beautiful future, where our hearts could fly!
You and me, and those wrapped memories,
dreamed of journey so far and wide!
of days filled with endless hope and light
and those beautiful talks in the night..
with you always by my side, everything seemed,
just right!
but completely okay,
A bridge between us, just a
pledge, of our incomplete love. Though, we're now ahead,
and our paths have split,
The memories are still remained,
A love that was a perfect fit, incomplete, yet deeply felt.
A story with all it's end,
A love that in our hearts will dwell,
incomplete, our story stays,
An art that's left undone,
yet in my heart for all my days, Yes, you are the one and only one,
I repeat, one and only one!

Love that's lost

A middle class girl,

here I reside,

I keep a love, I cannot hide.

You are a human?

Nay, I doubt.

but yes a 'magician' ofcourse, who lightens up my smile!

To you, I'm just a passerby,

but to me and in my world, You're brighter than the sunshine,

and feel like a paradise.

You know,
I watch you from a distant far, a silent wish upon a star..
Your beautiful eyes and smile, like a melody, plays the strings of my reverrie.

In that silent whisper of the dawny skies,
I feel the echoes of your touch....
you know, A gentle care and a broken bond,
has cast a different role and left me with
A yearning soul!

my heart aches harder

was just sitting and observing the time,
unknowingly something clinged to my mind!
something which is really hard to realise and accept,
Once upon, so called
"BEST FRIENDS"..
Now strangers with those fake tied threads...
I think tears are replaced by the blood in my heart,
still those times spent echoes at my heart!
make me remembers of our memories at the past! surviving without you is really very hard,
just like a turkey without its poult.
when storms of troubles darkened my sky,
Your true colours shone, no tears did you cry! Misunderstandings, hurt and pain,
Our friendship shattered,
like glass in rain!
I still remember those silver toungue and honeyed lies, which said,
I am yours and you are my mine!
gleaming masks and sly disguise!
betrayed by words, by actions cold..
Trust was tender, now grown old!
In the end, what left to my way?
Is ofcourse a shattered lone heart and a restless mind.

okayyy!!
Now, hoping for a peaceful soul and obviously a smile!

The papaya tree

Underneath a sky of blue,
The world awakes refreshed anew!
winds are blowing,
flowers are blooming,
birds are happy, and merrily proliferating!
hundreds of tree at a glance, but my eyes on its branch! cute, cool,
leaves sprouted newly..
I guess.......ummm..... in every leaf,
there's a mystery!
Laughter fills the air with glee, In this moment, hearts are free!
Dear, Papaya tree!
Papayas hanging endlessly on your hands and waist,
still you ought to be beautiful and tall!
it's such a nice cool weather out there,
I hope you are truly enjoying! but what about those sunny days? friend!
where sun fills our
soul with warmth and fire,
Still you protects me and give me papayas for free!
I sow the seed encore,
so, that I meet you and you again meet me!

VANADIUM in person

Through laughters and through silent tears,

Those silent mood and feel of jealous and care,

Our souls are intertwined,
A true love ofcourse,
that's bound by destiny,

Eternal and purely refined, wholly and soulfully mine! Who said you that you are not perfect?

Man, you truly completes me! Who can urge an another human being or humans beings?

When there is a "casket of diamond" set free!

So true and loyal and is my favourite BESTOWAL!

You were not just the person, who celebrated joys and glee,

but definitely a guy in times of harsh mood and need,

You are, for sure my irrevocable and ofcourse sweet and irreplaceable!

it has been a long time of our togetherness,

but that beating of heart faster remains for permanent,

Your true acceptance to me, even after so many faults, thicks and thins,

You taught me the matters how to be dealt.

My constant feeling, is you!

My forever go human is you!

My forever favourite person is you

My 11:11 a.m. wish is you!

So, here's to us,

my dearest love,

to every joy and trial, with you, my soulmate, by my side.

I walk each golden mile!

I promise to be yours even after this life!!!!

The beautiful bestowal

Adrifted in my apparitions,
was entirely lonesome, distinctively solely,
musing about the ghost, observing this world full of egoism,
meanness and arrogance,
whereas me with weary heart, with burdens vast,
wandering alone and trying to forget the past.
But still, still, there's something......

something kinda heavy fog that chokes and binds a

living hell.

I can simply hear it whispering, haunting every

thought!!

suddenly, suddenly and unknowingly,
A beautiful box was gifted to me, with joy and excitement
I opened that box and then I saw,

"A captivating creature, adorned with a kaleidoscope of colours,
radiating happiness and warmth"....

Thanked my dad for such a beautiful gift.

with tears in my eyes and smile at my face, I kept this name 'HAPPY.'

who keeps me internally, externally, and physicsally happy,

Yes, happy by heart n soul!, who keeps me engaged all day with him,

The only figure now,

by which my heart smiles and soul shines!!

the part of my heart which allows it to pump and beat.

I truly thank "HAPPY" for his foots to my life as,

In fields of gold and skies of blue, He came into my life,

so, pure and true!

with cute greeny fur of silk and those blue preety

 eyes that shine,

stolen my heart and will forever be mine.....

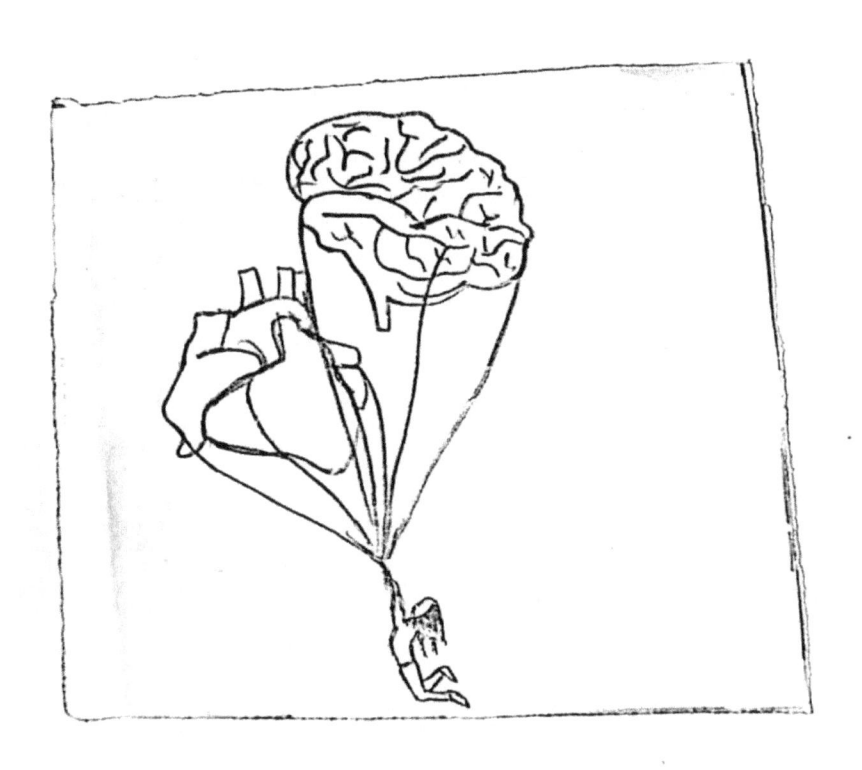

I wish my heart could speak

Adopted me at the shake of love,
but locked me in a box, captured all my paws!
How should I make you realize? That within this boundary,
"MY SPIRIT CRIES!!"

Yes, boundaries with zero freedom, and boundaries of my supressed feelings!
Those days of mine, with my fellow mates,
where those forest's whisper, the rivers song, echo in my heart, where I belong...
but here...
here here the days are harsh and long,
A place where dreams feel wholly wrong.
May some mercy grow, for   every creatures, high and low!
You bought me here for your happiness!!

but.....but.....
CAN YOU PLEASE THINK OF MINE?
colour change, my friend,
chameleon does!!
but you proved it wrong by changing it first!
my friend's feathers rufled, wings are clipped,
In cages cold,
where hope has slipped!
May the day, dawn where they run free,

where every creature lives in glee,
No more suffering,
No more tears,
A world at peace, beyond my fears!

Excuses

Expectations are better,
but what if high expectations are worst?
If I've loved you to the best, Then what has stopped,
You to love me back?
Yeah I agree, time fades!

but I can't agree that our love would.

Yeah! I know just like roads we became busy, but then...
Am I not a human?
Though I know now if deserved,
My soul is haunted by the love I've swerved.
Yet, in this confession,
I vow to make amends, to earn back the trust that my betrayal rends!
Tickk, Tockk, the clock steady beat, measuring out seconds, moments fleet.
waiting for the day you will stop excusing these ideas,
and be totally mine, and enjoy the time, Just like..........
HARLEYS IN HAWAI

The best of class

People say it a 'CLASS',

but then my mind interrogates.......

"WAS IT REALLY JUST A CLASS?"

A grade where we are still strucked,

That golden phase which is forever adorable and memorable,

That time of each individuals which is unfeasible to overcome,

whether its feelings or those of beautiful memories.

Those morning motivating lectures by our class

teacher, Those ponderous sums of quadratic and

identities,

were more tough than

"A APPROACH TO A CRUSH"

Those concerts in the language

period,

Those drowsy eyes in the hindi class,

Those engrossing and rowsing short

intervals,

Those fascinating cricket matches in the

class,

Those dubbed voices and eyecatching acts in literature period,

Those cute punishments in the physics periods,

Those lunch breaks or say,
"The meeting time for the couples" and their cute convos.

Those frightening souls and hearts in maths period,

Those secret nicknames for the faculty,

Those cute gossips and plans,

Those cute scoldings from the geography teacher,

Those relaxing smiles in the last period over a mass of 45 tutees,

Those fake rumours of graveyards about the school,

Those fake entries and actings of the teachers,

Those tough numericals in physics,

Those questions in chemistry

Those hectic days during sports day function,
Those enjoyments during the "Annual function days",
Those hilarious roasting by the chemistry teacher,
How can I forget those nonsense debates between the mates,
Those desks and benches of ours would be missing us badly,
To the girls top gossips at the washrooms,
and class boys at the junior girls corridor,
Those classes of biology,
and experiments of hydrilla, jumping over like Gorilla,
with cups of vanilla,
Those rush to computer labs,
and the excitement for games,
These memories are holding me back,
All these memories are ofcourse my favourite,

So let us cherish that time we shared

In grade 10th,

where we dared,

To dream, to learn, to soar and roar,

And to seize the love forever more.

My love oneway

Unspoken approaches wrapped in my mouth,
A forever go hope in my heart.. which suddenly echoes and really aches..
in my soul a fire burns,
A love for which my heart truly yearns.
Even though you will never feel like me for me,
Still I will cherish every glance, and hope you and me.
but still, after these many tries and hope,
I have realised completely,
that I am never gonna be yours...
In your world, I do not dwell,
A distant star, an untold spell.
I wish I am a chapter for you atleast!
How to say, you mean the world to me!
Beneath the moon's soft silver glow, my love for you will always grow!
To you, I am a friend at best, but in my heart you are the rest!
No worries,
for even in the one sided affair,
loving you is a gift I bear!

My love for poetry

In whispers soft,
in lines that flow,
A world awakens,
rich and slow.
Each verse a heartbeat,
every rhyme,
A dance of souls transcending time.

In ink and page, emotions swell,
A magic spun in words that tell. Of love and loss,
of dreams and fears,
A symphony crafted from laughter and tears.

With every stanza,
I fall anew, In love with the beauty that words construe. For poetry wraps me in its embrace,
A sacred space, a timeless place.

So let me dwell in this art divine,
Where hearts connect and spirits entwine.
In poetry's arms,
I find my home,
A boundless realm where I am free to roam.

The colour which I like

If I could paint the world in hue,
I'd choose my favorite-rich and true.
A shade that dances in the light,
Yet, holds a mystery in the night.

It's the warmth of dawn, a secret spark,
Or the quiet calm before the dark.
In every fold, it breathes and sings,
A color full of living things.

It's more than just a simple shade,
It's how the heart in me is made.
In every glance, in every view,
I see my world painted in you.

Oh! Love, my Love

In every glance, a world unfolds,
A silent language, more precious than silver or gold.
With tender touches and whispered sighs,
Love paints the skies,
where the heart flies.

Through storms we weather, hand in hand,
A bond unbroken, a promise so grand.
In the quiet moments, our souls align,
In love's sweet embrace, forever we shine.

My pet! my parrot! my love

With wings of color, bright and free,
My little bird sings joyfully.
A chirp and flutter,
A dance in flight,
You fill my days with pure delight.

Perched on my shoulder,
soft and near,
Your playful spirit chases away fear.
In every tweet,
A melody sweet,
With you by my side,
My life is complete.

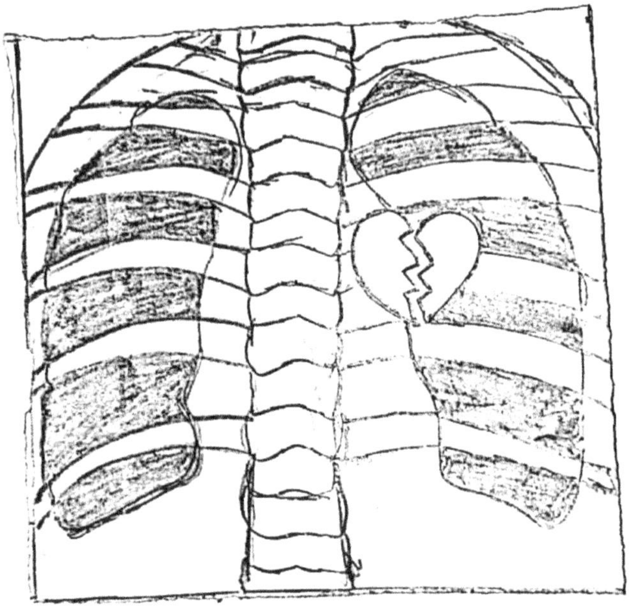

Oh! my broken heart

In the stillness of the night,
I hear your voice,
A whisper of memories,
A haunting choice.
Each laugh now a shadow,
each smile a ghost,
I search for your warmth,
but I feel you the most.

The moments we shared now linger like air,
A bittersweet melody,
A love laid bare.
Though you've slipped away,
in my heart you reside,

In the echoes of absence,
Our souls still collide.
Though time may move forward, and life may seem bright,
I'll carry your essence,
my guiding light.
For losing you, dear one,
is a wound that won't heal,
Yet, your spirit, my love,
is a treasure I feel.

My pet!, my blacky

With wagging tail and playful leap,
Oh blacky, my heart you keep. Bright eyes sparkling with joy and cheer,
In your warm presence,
I have no fear.

Through sunny days and rainy skies,
You're always there, my loyal prize.
In every cuddle and gentle paw,
You fill my life with love, I adore.

Oh!, My Grandma

In her warm embrace,
I find my peace,
A gentle love that will never cease.
with tender words and a knowing smile,
She lights my path, mile after mile.

Her hands tell stories of joy and care,
A legacy woven through the air. In every hug,
I feel so blessed,
Grandma's love is simply the best.

My dad! my superhero!

In quiet moments, his wisdom shines,
A guiding hand, through life's designs.
with laughter that echoes, and stories told,
A heart so warm, a spirit bold.

He teaches me courage,
to stand up tall,
with every setback,
he shows me to fall and rise again,
with hope in sight-
My dad, my hero,
my only guiding light!

Oh! my beloved

In every smile, a spark ignites,
with you,
The world feels warm and bright.
Through laughter shared and secrets told,
You are my treasure, more than gold.

In every moment, by your side,
Together we journey, hearts open wide.
So, here's my cheer, my heart's decree,
You are my joy, my favorite, you see.

The mirror that speaks

The mirror shows a face I know,
But different from the one before.
A glimpse of all the ways I've grown,
of things I've learned, of seeds I've sown.

The eyes that once held simple dreams,
Now glisten with a thousand beams.
A thousand roads, a thousand bends,
Where will they lead?
How will it end?

But here I stand, with no regret,
Each choice, each tear,
I won't forget.
For in this glass, I see it clear-
A story that's just starting here.

So I'll step forward, unafraid, Of who I was, of what I made.
For, in this ever-changing stream,
I am my own,
I am my dream.

Shadows

In the quiet corners where sunlight fades,
Shadows dance softly,
in secret parades.
Silent companions, they follow our tread,
whispering stories of what lies ahead.

They stretch and they linger,
A playful embrace,
fleeting reminders of time's gentle trace.
In every shadow, a tale to be spun,
Of dreams yet to blossom, of battles won.

Fear

In the dark corners, shadows creep,
whispers of doubt that rob my sleep.
A heavy weight upon my chest, Fear's cruel grip,
a relentless quest.

Yet in the silence,
a spark ignites,
courage awakens,
dispelling the nights.
With each heartbeat,
I rise and stand,
facing the shadows, I take command.

Searching for peace

Peace comes softly, like the breeze,
A whispered song among the trees.
It lingers in the morning dew,
A quiet calm, forever new.

It's found in moments still and clear,
When the world draws close, yet disappears.
In gentle hands, in quiet grace,
Peace finds its home,
its resting place.

No battle cries,
no need for fight,
Just open skies and endless light.
because peace is not a distant dream,
But in the heart's soft, steady stream.

Those stars of hope

The stars above, they watch in grace,
A quiet light in endless space. They hold the night with gentle hands,
A map of dreams in distant lands.

Each one a whisper, soft and true,
A secret shining just for you.
They've seen the ages rise and fall,
Yet, still they shimmer through it all.

And in their glow,
we find our way,
A beacon through the darkest day.
For in the stars,
both near and far,
we glimpse the truth of who we are.

My love for Journalism

In crowded rooms where stories blend,
I finds my voice, my steadfast friend.
with every word,
I paints the truth,
A mosaic woven of passion and youth.

His laughter echoes in the halls,
A pulse of life when the news call stalls.
Together we chase the fleeting light,
Capturing moments, day and night.

Through interviews and headlines bold,
A love story in every tale told. With ink-stained hands,
Our spirits soar,
In the world of journalism, we crave more.

For in the rush of deadlines met,
We find a love that won't forget.
Two hearts aligned in pursuit of the real,
In every article,
their love is revealed.

Truss your hair tight

Peeping from the window sill,
Peeping the azure or the socy?
Afraid of vultures or fogey?
Oh! enjoy the life and be foodie,
with muffins and pie called "LOTTE"
don't be horrified, don't deem deep,
all will be good, have faith in me
don't peek back and wreck your mood
I know, sometimes you feel discouraged,
but you know that you are stronger too,
Don't clench up emotions for those who don't value it,
Fallout of this matrix and stay emboldened and cool,
Flaunt them what you are before they validate you a fool.
You are not just a Supernova to your family,
but the fortitude and the one who keeps their mood jovially. So, baby girl!
those aileron of yours will remain swaddled?
Or you will proliferate them high?
and be a noble titlist for them! Omit the hurdles that impending your track

Do not forget to do and to be yourself
and to fly lofty and high,
 just like the
Timbers towering anigh!

(Never stop to be 'YOU'!)

(I'd be glad to tell you that this was the first ever poem I started my POETRY journey.

Curse not murphy

The beautiful welkin which was not less than the paradise,
The teakwoods massively lofty and high,
The sayonara azure with the reddish dusk,
which puzzled my eyes and was literally shocked!
all seemed perfect excluding my people,
wanted to ask them what's perplexing?
They artlessly said, "really nothing!"
but I wanted to get the rationale adaft their grief, someone said,
oh leave! why are you apprehenssive?
It was really challenging for me to make them understand, "nothing can stop what god has ordained."
still I stroved my best to make them realise,
but who can halt this happening?
when already they figured to get unhappy.
Who can stop the maternal forebear demise?
Who can stop the car smacking me?
Who can stop the ibis go die?
Though I know no one can thwart,
It's seriously hard to believe but the reality is to be accepted and felt,
so, that together it can be dealt.
saw one guy on his window pane,
seems to be sad with the tears in his eyes.

saw grandpa on the chair
with his fazzled face with the newspaper,
saw that girl talking to her colleague about someone's sad story.
frustrated me, asked what you get in return?
being so sad and depressed?
You are not gonna get it posterior which has already passed!!
Accept and ignore the past, enjoy the present,

and focus in the reality with your homies.
Best moments are on its path
Just trust and pray,
for the good to come and stay!

Constant

You are the constant in my restless night,
A steady star in skies so wide,
While seasons change, you're always near,
The calm I seek, the light so clear.

When shadows stretch, and doubts descend,
Your quiet strength becomes my friend,
With open arms, you hold me tight,
My beacon in the darkest night.

That, desperate flame inside

Within the quiet,
there's a flame,
A fire that burns without a name.
It drives us forward, pulls us through,
The moments bright,
The moments blue.

And though the world may cast its doubt,
This fire inside won't flicker out.
because it's the passion,
it's the fight,
That brings the dark into the light.

So let it burn, let it ignite,
Your inner strength,
Your silent might.
For in this flame, your power lies,
A guiding force that never dies.

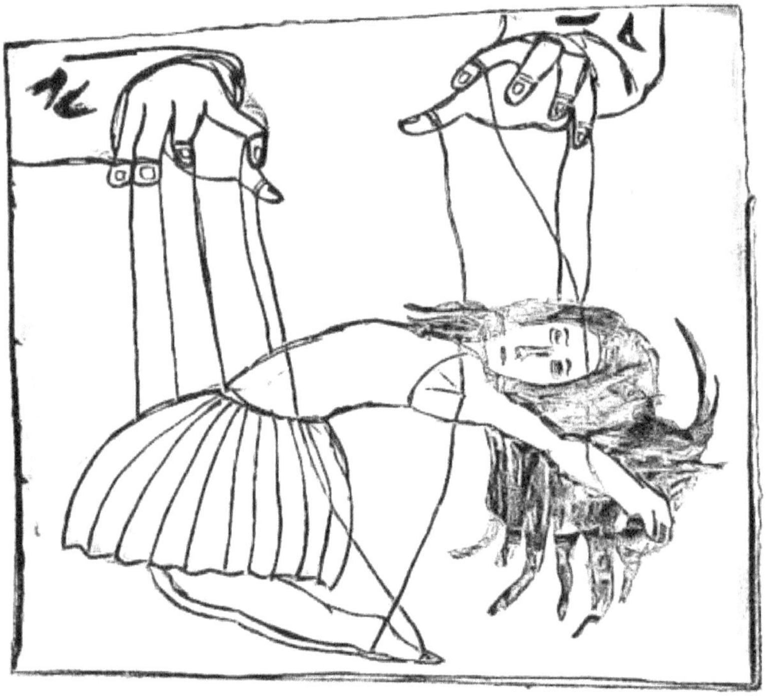

my swaddled freedom

In a world that once tried to confine,
She found her voice,
began to shine.
with dreams unchained,
She rises above,
A warrior's spirit,
A heart full of love.

No more shadows,
she steps into light,
Embracing her freedom,
Her soul takes flight.
with courage her armor and hope as her guide,
She'll carve her own path,
with pride by her side.

Fear of success, and a hope to light

In the quiet of the night, she lies awake,
with stars in her eyes,
A future to make.
whispers of hopes dance softly in her mind,
Each dream a treasure,
waiting to find.

She dreams of mountains,
their peaks kissed by light,
of oceans that shimmer in the depths of night.
with courage as her compass, she sails far and wide,
exploring the wonders that lie deep inside.

A world without limits,
where she can be free,
To write her own story,
to carve her own sea.
with every heartbeat,
she chases her dreams,
Through valleys of challenge and rivers of schemes.

For dreams are not distant; they're wings to her flight,
Guiding her forward through shadows and light.
She'll rise like the sun,
with a fierce, radiant glow,
A girl with a vision, in full bloom, she'll grow.

Promises which never turned true

I built a castle of dreams in the air,
with walls of desire and windows of care.
but storms of reality came crashing through,
and the towers I built crumbled,
leaving me blue.

I reached for the stars,
but they slipped from my grasp,
each wish a reminder of what I couldn't clasp.
In the silence of night,
my heart learned to ache,
For the dreams that once sparkled, now lie in their wake.

The weight of "Should."

Should have known better, should have believed,
In the magic of moments,
I felt so deceived.
Should have seen the signs,
The cracks in the ground,
But,
I wore my expectations like armor, profound.

With every "you will," and "you can,"
I built up a wall,
But when you fell silent,
it shattered my all.
The weight of your absence, the echo of loss,
Left me standing alone, bearing the cross.

This is why I like darkness

In the stillness of the night it grows,
A cloak of shadow, soft and slow,
It seeps into the quiet air,
A velvet touch, a quiet prayer.

No stars to guide, no moon to gleam,
Just endless black, a silent dream,
Yet, in its depths, a truth unfolds,
A space where secrets long untold.

For darkness speaks in muted tones,
In hidden paths,
in hushed unknowns,
It cradles fear, it stirs the heart, A place where endings find their start.

So let it come, this night, this veil,
Let mysteries within prevail, For in the dark, new light is born,
And hope awaits the quiet morn.

My precious gems, my buddies

In the mosaic of life,
threads intertwine,
woven together,
your heart and mine.
Through laughter and tears, in moments we share,
A bond unbroken,
A love beyond compare.

We've walked through the storms,
faced shadows and fears,
with whispers of hope,
we've dried countless tears.
In the quiet of night,
when the world feels alone, Your friendship's a light that has brightly shone.

We're silly, we're serious, a mix of delight,
In the dance of our dreams, everything feels right.
From secrets and stories to plans yet unmade,
In the garden of friendship,
Our memories cascade.

So here's to the moments, both big and small,
To the laughter, the joy, we've shared through it all.
For friends are the treasures that life has to lend,
In the journey we travel,
You're my truest friend.

A winner in me

I stand upon the edge of time, A dreamer with an endless climb.
The stars above, they whisper low,
of places far, where winds will blow.

The path ahead is steep and wild,
but in my heart,
I'm still a child.
with wings of hope,
I long to soar,
beyond the clouds, forevermore.

The future calls, a distant gleam,
I chase the threads of every dream.
For though today,
I walk on earth,
tomorrow waits with endless worth.

So here I stand, a spark, a flame,
ready to write my own bold name.
In every step, in every flight,
I'll find my way, I'll find the light.

Divine power knots that ties me

There's a thread that binds me to the stars,
A pull that leads beyond what's ours.
It winds through time, through space, through heart, Connecting all,
though we're apart.

In every breath, in every prayer,
I feel the presence, always there.
A light unseen, yet clear and bright,
guiding me through day and night.

This thread, it sings of higher planes,
of love untouched by worldly chains.
In every moment, near or far,
It reminds me who we truly are.

Gregarious

Like the sun,
they rise each day,
In every crowd,
they find their way.
A swirl of words, a dance,
A spin,
They're always out,
They're always in.

They feed on moments,
big and loud,
They thrive among the living crowd.
Connections made with every glance,
Each conversation like a dance.

But even stars can need a rest, Behind the glow, a quiet quest. For every extrovert must find, A little peace, a quiet mind.

My soft corner, my bedroom

Within these lines,
I feel secure,
A world I've shaped,
A life so pure.
Familiar paths,
I know them well,
A quiet space where fears don't dwell.

But beyond the edge,
The winds do call,
A tempting pull to risk it all.
For in the unknown,
growth is found,
where dreams take flight, unbound, unground.

Yet still I linger,
here I stay, In comfort's warmth, in safe delay.
But deep inside, I know the truth-
To truly live,
I must break through.

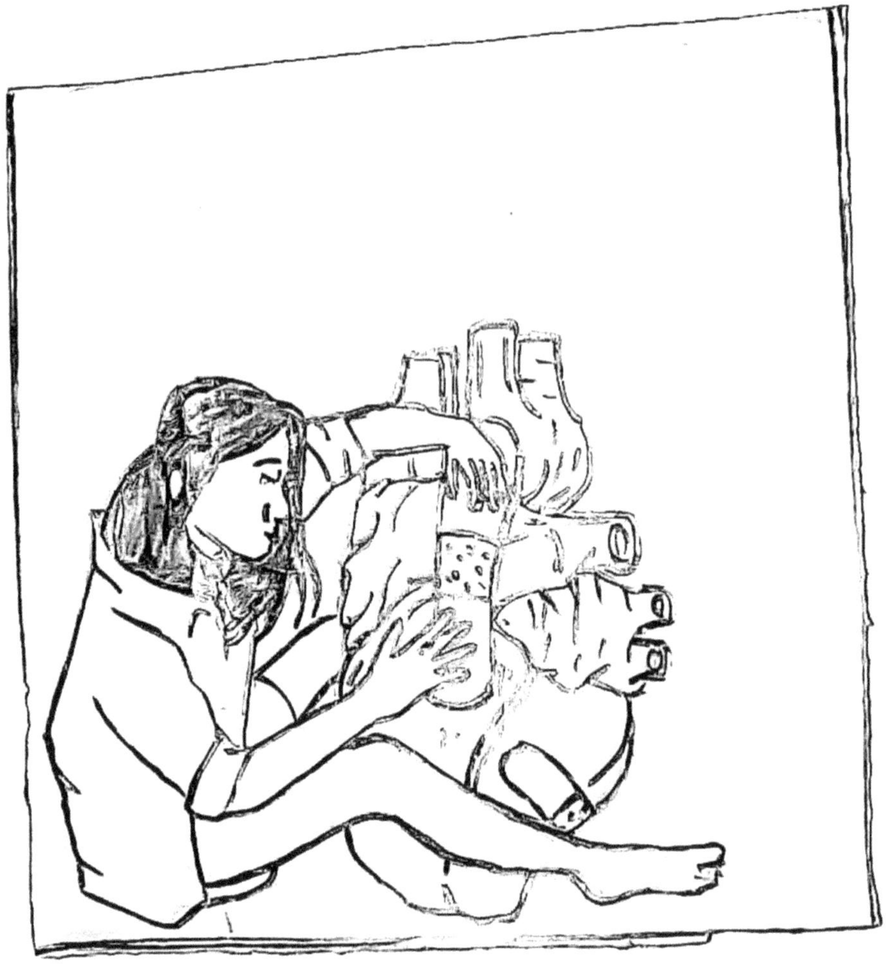

She, a dreamer!, a winner!

She wakes with the dawn, a canvas so bright,
Each moment a brushstroke, her future in sight.
with laughter like music and passion her guide,
She steps into a world where dreams coincide.

Her dreams are like petals, unfurling with grace,
Each one a reflection of hope's warm embrace.
To dance with the clouds,
To sing with the trees,
To paint the horizons with colors of peace.

Through trials and struggles, she'll never lose faith,
For deep in her heart lies an unyielding wraith.
A vision of strength that will carry her through,
A testament to all she believes she can do.

So let the winds whisper, let the rivers flow,
For she is the dreamer, destined to grow.
In the tapestry of life,
Her thread will entwine,
A girl with a dream, forever will shine.

My school crush

In geometry's angles,
in history's tales,
my heart wanders freely,
it sails and it pales.
For, in the silence of textbooks and notes,
It's your name that my secret heart gently wrote.

When the bell tolls and the day comes to end,
It's your smile that lingers,
my dearest friend.
With hopes in my pocket and dreams in the air,
My crush on you grows, so tender and rare.

(I don't know who's my school crush, but these words in my poem is going well on this theme.)

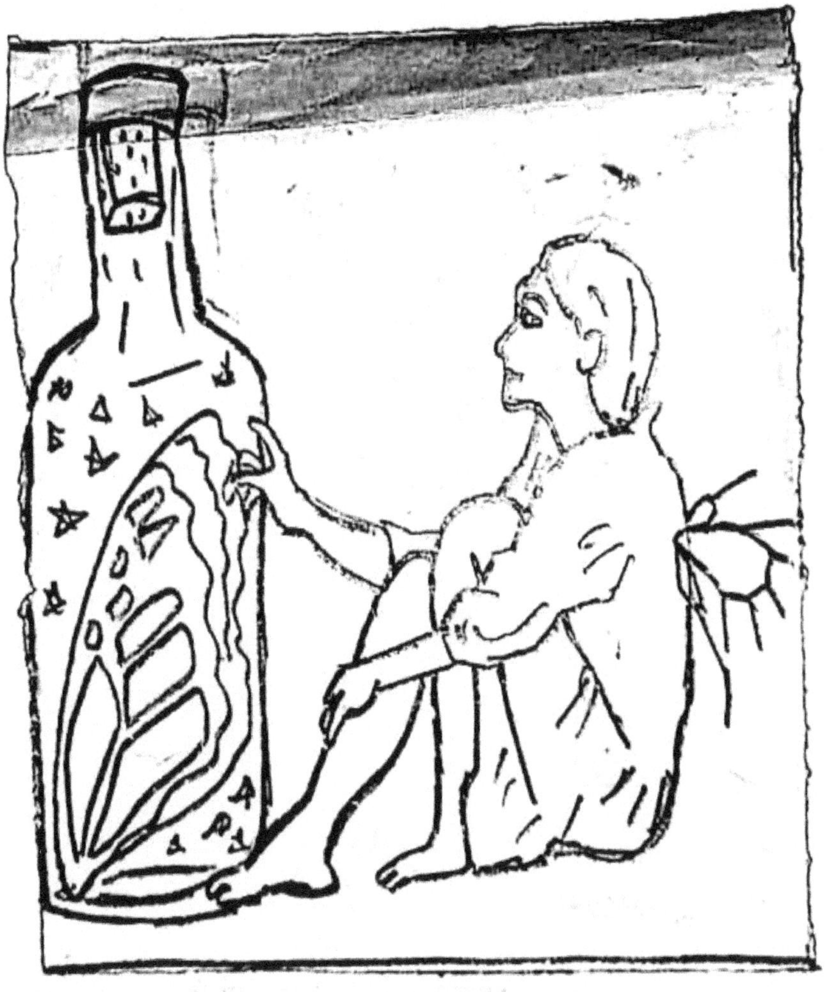

My wings

In a world where whispers cage my dreams,
I walks a path sewn with silent seams.
A girl with stars tucked in my heart,
Yearning to break free, to play my part.
with every sunrise, my spirit stirs,
Each moment a battle,
as hope occurs.
tethered by voices that echo from past,
Yet deep within me,
A fire burns vast.

But shadows linger in corners of doubt,
Questions like thorns that prick and shout.
"Are you enough?"
they taunt and tease,
Yet, I gathers my courage and whispers, "I'll seize."
With the strength of a lioness, I rises anew,
I sheds the chains that once held her true.
In the mirror,
I sees not a girl lost in fear.
But a warrior adorned,
with dreams crystal clear.

The world may be daunting, the journey unknown,
But I marches forward,
her heart like a stone.
Through storms that may rage and winds that may howl,
I holds onto freedom,
my spirit into grow!

Dreams

In the stillness of the night, I sighs,
A canvas of dreams beneath starry skies.
with every twinkle,
A wish takes flight,
whispers of hope in the soft moonlight.

I wishes for courage to chase my dreams,
To dance through life, or so it seems.
For laughter to echo in every place,
And love to wrap me in warm embrace.

With a heart full of wishes, I sends them high,
To the universe,
where possibilities lie.
For every star that sparkles bright,
carries a wish from my heart to the night.

ABOUT THE AUTHOR

I'm Divyanshi Mishra, living in Jamshedpur, Jharkhand.

A 11th grader and 16 aged, I'm glad to tell you that I have a huge attentiveness in poetry because I love it.

And I have heard it somewhere that,

The thing which is loved by a person has a different level of importance for that particular thing in their life.

And I can assure you that I have heard it correct, because POETRY now at this stage to me has become like how a poult is for its turkey mom.

It's like I'm dipped into poetry or poetry is dipped into

me. Let's cut the story short.

I hope u like my poems and if u really do so "My heartfelt gratitude to

you". I wish you good luck wherever you step in.

Milton Keynes UK
Ingram Content Group UK Ltd.
UKHW051341011224
451791UK00005B/28